"Rick Johnson expresses what millions of us see and feel today when it comes to broken male culture and the absence of models and mentors to train the next generation of men. The void is titanic. But instead of glorifying the pain and connected issues like most of the media hyenas do, *A Man in the Making* goes to the root—helping dads see what makes truly great men by studying the greats. I believe that new personal and family histories await the men who see and internalize the timeless observations contained in this treasure chest of manhood."

—**Kenny Luck**, author of *Sleeping Giant*,
pastor of men at Saddleback Church,
and founder of Every Man Ministries

"I am so grateful for friends like Rick Johnson who diligently expose me to models and pathways and illustrations of how I can launch my three boys into godly adulthood. This is my job and I cannot and I must not give it away to another!"

—**Brian Doyle**, founder and president
of Iron Sharpens Iron

A MAN
in the
MAKING

A MAN
in the
MAKING

Strategies to Help
YOUR SON
Succeed in Life

RICK JOHNSON

Revell
a division of Baker Publishing Group
Grand Rapids, Michigan

Published by Revell
a division of Baker Publishing Group
P.O. Box 6287, Grand Rapids, MI 49516-6287
www.revellbooks.com

Printed in the United States of America

Library of Congress Cataloging-in-Publication Data
Johnson, Rick, 1956–
    A man in the making : strategies to help your son succeed in life / Rick Johnson.
        pages cm
    Includes bibliographical references.
    ISBN 978-0-8007-2032-2 (pbk.)
    1. Men—Conduct of life. 2. Character. 3. Virtues. 4. Men—Biography.
5. Child rearing—Religious aspects—Christianity. 6. Parent and child—Religious aspects—Christianity. I. Title.
BJ1601.J64 2013
248.8′45—dc23   2013013663

Scripture quotations labeled KJV are from the King James Version of the Bible.

Scripture quotations labeled NIV are from the Holy Bible, New International Version®. NIV®. Copyright © 1973, 1978, 1984, 2011 by Biblica, Inc.™ Used by permission of Zondervan. All rights reserved worldwide. www.zondervan.com

Scripture quotations labeled NIV 1984 are from the Holy Bible, New International Version®. NIV®. Copyright © 1973, 1978, 1984 by Biblica, Inc.™ Used by permission of Zondervan. All rights reserved worldwide. www.zondervan.com

Scripture quotations labeled NKJV are from the New King James Version. Copyright © 1982 by Thomas Nelson, Inc. Used by permission. All rights reserved.

Scripture quotations labeled NLT are from the Holy Bible, New Living Translation, copyright © 1996, 2004, 2007 by Tyndale House Foundation. Used by permission of Tyndale House Publishers, Inc., Carol Stream, Illinois 60188. All rights reserved.

13 14 15 16 17 18 19   7 6 5 4 3 2 1

To two special men—
one who *will* make a difference,
and one who *did*:

To George—
God has BIG plans for you, my friend.

To Dr. Edward M. Scott (RIP)—
you never knew how much difference you made,
and I'm still finding out.
Thank you.

Contents

Still I have a favor to ask of them. When my sons are grown up, I would ask you, O my friends, to punish them; and I would have you trouble them, as I have troubled you, if they seem to care about riches, or anything, more than about virtue; or if they pretend to be something when they are really nothing—then reprove them, as I have reproved you, for not caring about that for which they ought to care, and thinking that they are something when they are really nothing. And if you do this, both I and my sons will have received justice at your hands.

—Socrates, upon being sentenced to death for "corrupting the minds of the youth of Athens"

"Carter had things like honor, things like valor. He was noble. Those used to be good words, right? But somehow they got . . . stupid-sounding, you know? Kind of—*ugh*—heavy and overbearing and even comical. How does that happen to a word? He can look on the TV"—she was talking about the boy now—"he can look at the TV, he'll see all these men struttin' around, all muscle and gold and guns. Struttin' around like they somethin' fine, like they tough, you know? Talkin' about slappin' they hos. Carter was nothing like that. Carter was a *man*. He treated me like . . ." She didn't finish. She fought back her tears. She shook her head. "Even the word *man*," she said. "How does that happen to a word?"

—Andrew Klavan, *The Identity Man*

I want to play a real man in all my films and I define manhood simply: men should be tough, fair, and courageous, never petty, never looking for a fight, but never backing down from one either.

—John "Duke" Wayne

Boys to Men

OVER THE YEARS IT HAS BEEN MY PERSONAL MISSION to advocate the importance of men and fathers in families, within communities, and around the world. I truly believe God anointed me with that message and has given me the ability and vehicles—my books and speaking ministry—to share it.

Because of my background, I have always been fascinated with what authentic masculinity looks like, its power to influence, and how it is acquired or transferred during the transition from boyhood to manhood.

After years of research, observation and study, real-life experiences, and operating ministry programs (such as mentoring fatherless boys, leading father-son campouts, and working with men in virtually every venue from churches to prisons), I have come to the conclusion that healthy masculinity is a somewhat fragile gift that must be intentionally passed down from one generation of men to the next. Any misstep or break in that transference can lead to a corruption of the process, resulting in skewed and damaged men. And damaged men typically do not make good leaders, husbands, or fathers.

Early last year I was convicted by God that while I was reaching thousands, perhaps tens of thousands, of men and boys each year with my books and my speaking ministry, my influence in their lives was somewhat wide and shallow. Even though I want to continue *those* efforts, I was compelled to start sharing my experience and knowledge through a deeper but narrower focus by individually mentoring young men. While I initially entered into that endeavor with some trepidation, it has turned out to be a truly invigorating experience. I currently mentor a young man from Nigeria in his mid-twenties whose parents were tragically killed when he was seventeen. His eagerness to learn about what it means to be a man and a leader has blessed me as much or more than our work together has benefited him. It has caused me to actually think about the process of becoming a healthy man and what teachings and experiences are important to be included in that process.

This experience has reinforced my belief that it requires a plan and a good deal of intentionality to effectively raise a boy to become a healthy man and leader. Without a plan and intentional effort, we settle for whatever we get. Let me give you an example. I married my wife because, not only was she incredibly hot looking, but she's such a fantastic cook that she could cook my garbage and make it taste good. But because of that, she doesn't always follow a recipe (a plan) for the meals she cooks. Most of the time this works out great and we have an excellent meal. Every so often, however, things don't quite work out as well as they could have. Thankfully, I'll eat about anything as long as it has meat in it, so it hasn't ever been too big of an issue. But her proficiency in her cooking abilities sometimes encourages her to be overconfident, and the result sometimes leaves something to be desired. In other words, her meals in those rare circumstances do not reach their full potential.

The same goes for making boys into men. When we don't have a plan—a recipe to follow—they *might* turn out great or they might turn out as men with something to be desired. Regardless, they seldom reach their full potential without a plan.

We are currently facing the phenomena of having a large percentage of our young males who have not had positive male role models intentionally bringing them into manhood. We are bereft of healthy male leadership in our culture today. As a result, we are seeing these boy-men delaying adulthood, underachieving, not going to college, being unemployed or underemployed, creating and abandoning children, and generally being unprepared to meet the world. I was raised in an alcoholic home with all the disadvantages that environment brings with it. I was raised to believe that religion was a crutch for weak people and that all Christians were hypocrites. By the age of forty, after attaining all that the world says should make you happy and successful, I found myself yearning for more. Something was missing. I had a hole in my soul that could not be filled by success, achievement, or materialistic acquisition. That chasm in my soul was destroying me.

In an attempt to find inner satisfaction and peace, I studied a number of religions and belief systems. Since at the time I did not have any real friends or other men I looked up to for advice, I decided to look at the lives of men throughout history whom I admired to see what they had that made them significant. Interestingly, the only common denominator I discovered between all these great and admirable men was the fact that they were all Christians—men of great faith. That epiphany was a mighty blow to the worldview I had been raised with. I personally had always been a bit contemptuous of Christianity. At the very least it just seemed inconsequential or insignificant in the bigger picture of things. I wasn't necessarily hostile toward it; I just thought it was a misguided philosophy designed and developed by perhaps earnest but intellectually weak or even ignorant men thousands of years ago to keep uneducated and ambitionless people content with their lot in life. Sort of along the lines of Karl Marx's quote, "Religion is the opium of the people."

However, upon making this discovery, I began to investigate the history and doctrinal foundations of Christianity. I set out upon a yearlong study of anthropologic, geologic, and historical components of Scripture in order to disprove the validity of the Gospels. After that year I came to the conclusion that not only could I *not* disprove the truth of the Gospels, but that they were in fact true. After accepting Christ as my Savior, I felt a huge sense of peace, satisfaction, contentment, and most of all forgiveness that cannot be described or proven by any scientific method I'm aware of. I just knew in my soul that this was *truth* in its purest form. I felt fulfilled and whole. This then propelled me into the work I do today, which has allowed me to lead a much more fulfilling life than I ever thought possible.

The study of great men throughout history was what initially led me to be interested in pursuing salvation. Was it coincidence that every historically significant man I happened to study was a Christian? Probably not. But as I have investigated and researched further, it appears to be extremely difficult to find *any* men throughout history who have made a positive and significant difference in the world who were not Christians or at least men of great faith. (For example, someone such as Mahatma Gandhi could probably be considered a man who made a significant, positive difference in the world and, though not a Christian, had a deep religious and moral faith.) C. S. Lewis explains it this way: "I am very doubtful whether history shows us one example of a man who, having stepped outside traditional morality and attained power, has used that power benevolently."[1]

With that in mind I have used great men throughout history and the character traits they were most famous for to illustrate the foundations we need to instill in young men in order to develop healthy and truly life-giving masculinity. Were these men perfect? No. They were ordinary human beings like you and me—flawed, imperfect, and prone to making mistakes. But they did not allow those imperfections to keep them from changing the world for the better.

Too many men in our culture either use the power of their masculinity to do harm or they neglect and waste it. If we are to teach boys and young men to wisely use the power God has endowed them with by virtue of their gender, we must be intentional. If we are to teach them to use that power to bless the lives of others, we must proactively develop and implement a plan, not just hope and pray for a positive outcome.

In the early nineteenth century, an idea called the Great Man Theory developed to describe how "great men"—through their personal attributes, such as charisma, intelligence, wisdom, or political skill—used their power to significantly influence history. A proponent of that theory, British essayist and historian Thomas Carlyle, believed great men—heroes—helped to make history with not just those personal attributes, but also with the help of God.[2]

For purposes of this book, I chose a number of men of faith whose lives were significant and who impacted the lives of many others. All of these men led exemplary lives on some level—not perfect, but significant. Each chapter contains a short bio on the man and how he exhibited the character trait he was known for, a section on why that specific trait is important to teach your son, and finally some practical ways to intentionally instill that character trait into your son's life. These character traits are not in any particular order of importance, although I did try to put similar traits together in the chapter order.

These traits are not the only traits our boys need to learn, but they are a good starting point to begin to intentionally develop a plan to proactively teach our sons to become leaders and good men.

Additionally, you'll notice that I did not discuss specific moral values such as sexual purity, honesty, faithfulness, or fidelity—not because they are not important, but rather I had hoped that parents who were interested in raising boys with strong character would instinctively know that a strong moral foundation is the essence of all character. Also, I did not discuss developing faith or spirituality within your son. Again, not because I do not believe it is vitally important, but because I wanted this book to be one that will reach parents of all faith walks and belief systems. I wanted the focus to be on raising sons to become good men, not necessarily "religious" ones.

That said, all parents must have faith on some level or another. Faith is not the absence of doubt but persevering despite our doubts, just as courage is not the absence of fear but continuing on despite our fears. We need to have the courage to raise men of great faith and character. Our culture is at a crossroads. We need great men to once again lead and shape our culture through strong character and divine inspiration. I don't think it's any coincidence that only a few of the men I refer to in this book have been alive in the last forty years or so. We create great men by intentionally growing them from boys. As you go through this book, keep your eye on the ultimate goal—to create men who will change history. Without those great men . . . may God help us all.

1

Courage

Martin Luther King Jr.

Courage is rightly esteemed the first of human qualities because it is the quality which guarantees all others.

—Winston Churchill

COURAGE IS THE QUALITY OF MIND OR SPIRIT THAT ENABLES a person to face uncertainty, difficulty, intimidation, danger, or pain with or without fear. In fact, true courage may be doing something we fear despite our fear. Courage is also generally considered interchangeable with bravery, which is the ability to stand up for what is right in difficult situations. Boldness, fearlessness, mettle, and fortitude are also considered to be courageous qualities.

Courage, according to Aristotle, is in between fear and recklessness. Cowards shrink from things they shouldn't be afraid of, and reckless men take unnecessary risks because they are overly confident. True courage requires us to act courageously despite our fears.[1]

Courage can be exhibited in one of two ways—moral courage is the ability to do the right thing even when faced with popular opposition, discouragement, or shame. Physical courage is courage in the face of pain, hardship, or threat.

Millions of men throughout history have exhibited courage in one way or another. But I believe one man exhibited both of those forms of courage better than perhaps anyone else.

Dr. Martin Luther King Jr.—Courage in the Face of Adversity

Dr. Martin Luther King Jr. (1929–1968) was a Baptist minister and prominent leader of the African-American civil rights movement. Influenced by the teachings of Mahatma Gandhi, he believed strongly in nonviolent social change. In 1964, King became the youngest person to receive the Nobel Peace Prize for his work to end racial segregation and racial discrimination through civil disobedience and other nonviolent means.

Growing up in Atlanta, King excelled in school, skipping both the ninth and the twelfth grade before entering Morehouse College at age fifteen without formally graduating from high school. In 1948, he graduated from Morehouse and enrolled in Crozer Theological Seminary, from which he graduated with a Bachelor of Divinity degree in 1951. King became pastor of the Dexter Avenue Baptist Church in Montgomery, Alabama, in 1954 when he was twenty-five years old. King then began doctoral studies at Boston University and received his Doctor of Philosophy in 1955.

Dr. King maintained a policy of not publicly endorsing a US political party or candidate, believing "someone must remain in the position of nonalignment, so that he can look objectively at both parties and be the conscience of both—not the servant or master of either."[2]

Despite harassment from the FBI, King was convinced that nonviolent protests against Jim Crow laws would eventually create a wave of sympathy from the public. This strategy helped make civil rights the most important issue of the early 1960s.

Dr. King's main strategy was to organize and lead nonviolent marches to bring light upon issues such as blacks' right to vote, desegregation, labor rights, and other civil rights.

Protests in Birmingham began with a boycott to pressure businesses to offer sales jobs and other employment to people of all races, as well as to end segregated facilities in the stores. When business leaders resisted the boycott, King and his group began what they termed Project C, a series of sit-ins and marches intended to provoke arrest. During the protests, the Birmingham Police Department, led by Eugene "Bull" Connor, used high-pressure water jets and police dogs to control protesters, including children. King was originally criticized for using children in the protest. But by the end of the campaign, King's reputation was cemented, Connor lost his job, the Jim Crow signs were removed, and public places became more open to blacks.

Dr. King also participated in a number of high-profile marches and demonstrations, the most famous possibly being the March on Washington. The march originally was conceived to bring to light the desperate condition of blacks in the southern United States. The march made specific demands to the government including an end to racial segregation in public schools; meaningful civil rights legislation, including a law prohibiting racial discrimination in employment; protection of civil rights workers from police brutality; a two-dollar minimum wage for all workers. Despite tensions between the organizing factions, the march was a big success. More than a quarter million people of diverse ethnicities attended the event; at the time, it was the largest gathering of protesters in Washington's history.

King wrote powerfully and delivered a number of famous speeches that are still relevant and inspirational today. Dr. King's brilliant "Letter from Birmingham Jail," written in 1963, is a passionate statement of his crusade for justice. I recommend you get a copy and read it aloud with your son—you will both have goose bumps. Then take it apart paragraph by paragraph and study what Dr. King says; there are some fascinating insights and words of wisdom contained in this letter.

His seventeen-minute "I Have a Dream" speech, delivered on August 28, 1963, called for racial equality and an end to discrimination. Along with Abraham Lincoln's Gettysburg Address and Franklin D. Roosevelt's Infamy Speech, it is considered one of the finest speeches in the history of American oratory. On April 3, 1968, the day before his death, King delivered his famous "I've Been to the Mountaintop" address at a rally.

Dr. King was assassinated by a gunman on April 4, 1968, in Memphis, Tennessee, on the second-floor balcony outside his hotel room. He was posthumously awarded the Presidential Medal of Freedom in 1977 and the Congressional Gold Medal in 2004. Martin Luther King Jr. Day was established as a US federal holiday in 1986.

Like all the men in this book, Dr. King was a courageous, yet all-too-human male. Even with his faults, he never wavered in the courage and conviction of his faith. Dr. King had to know from early in his career that he was in danger of bodily harm or death. He received hundreds, perhaps thousands, of death threats; he was continually harassed; he was arrested multiple times; and he was subjected to intense pressure and stress. And yet that did not stop him from pursuing a noble goal—one that ultimately changed the lives of millions of people and made the world a better place. That kind of courage and commitment is rare today, which makes it even more important.[3]

Why Courage Is Important

Brave men are vertebrates; they have their softness on the surface and their toughness in the middle. But these modern cowards are all crustaceans; their hardness is all on the cover and their softness is inside.

—G. K. Chesterton

Courage is one of the greatest virtues a man and a leader can have. Aristotle listed it as the top virtue of all in his famous work, *Nicomachean Ethics*. It is virtually impossible to be an effective leader without courage. Leading a family, operating a business, going to school, and even volunteering your time require courage in various degrees.

Unfortunately, it is difficult being a man in today's culture. The definition of manhood is evolving with no clear boundaries. Masculinity is devalued and even mocked in our feminized culture. (Just look how men are portrayed on sitcoms or in movies.) Not only that, but it is difficult being a husband and a father. Many women seem to *want* men to lead their families—as long as they lead them the way a woman would. Men get a lot of criticism (and rightfully so) for the problems they cause but seldom get much credit for what they are doing right. All that to say, it takes courage to stand by your convictions—to do what is right when those around you think you are wrong. It takes courage to risk being criticized. Generally, when men of conviction take a stand, many factions of our culture are quick to attack them. You can find many examples of this—from men who operate the Boy Scouts of America and refuse to allow homosexuals to infiltrate their leadership ranks, to men who try to pray in public. Those men are viciously attacked in the media. Any time you go against the prevailing wisdom of a culture you are subject to attack. It doesn't mean you are wrong and society is right.

Courage is not the absence of fear but the conquest of it. Courage (especially in males) is the willingness to fail. Courage is the defender and protector of all other virtues. It is essential in order to guard the best qualities of the soul and to clear their way for action. To be afraid to the point of paralysis is to have no soul. But courage emancipates us and allows us to move with freedom and vigor. Author and educator Henry Van Dyke described the effect of courage: "Not to tremble at the shadows which surround us, not to shrink from the foes who threaten us, not to hesitate and falter and stand despairing still among the perplexities and trials of life, but to move steadily onward without fear."[4] When parents exhibit courage, they produce children with courage. Billy Graham once noted, "Courage is contagious. When a brave man takes a stand, the spines of others are often stiffened."[5]

Teach your son that being "nice" isn't the highest aspiration a man can live up to. (Mom, I know this goes against your nature, but bear with me.) In fact, sometimes I think niceness is the enemy of courage. Many times in life a man, husband, or father is forced to make decisions in the best interest of his family or society that do not appear to be nice on the outside. I've been forced as a father to make decisions that my children perceived at the time as heartless, mean-spirited, or just plain stupid. But they were always made with their best interest in the long run in mind. If my goal had only been to be nice (or to have been liked), I would not have been able to make the hard decisions that were important to their long-term healthy growth and development.

Our culture promotes being nice as the highest virtue a man can achieve. It is easier to drift along with the current of the culture than to try to swim against it. Many of the newer "guy" movies inspire males to be lovable, nice slackers, with no aim in life but to smoke pot, bed women, and get by without working. But the young men are very "nice," so it's okay. And many young women today seem drawn to soft, passive, quiet men who do not ruffle feathers and who do what they are told. It's a nonthreatening but uninspired vision of manhood.

Niceness and meanness are feminine concepts. You seldom see men complaining that another man is mean or not nice. On the outside, that desire for niceness in males would appear to be a noble goal. However, it's really a way of neutering masculinity. Being nice takes away the power of a man to lead. It removes passion, conviction, and courage from a man's soul. Nice guys might not always finish last, but they seldom run the race at all.

I recently had a discussion with two men—one older and one younger than me—about a recent church upheaval. They were both very "nice" guys. The older man made the comment that he really didn't want to know the details behind what was happening because then he would be forced to make a judgment. The young man agreed and said he would rather not have to face the problems because then he would be forced to choose a side. I was shocked and not a little disgusted by their responses. They'd rather stick their heads in the sand than have to take a stand and be perceived as being judgmental. They lacked the courage to stand up for what they believe in. When did *judging* the value of anything become such a sin in our culture anyway? Anything except whether a person is nice or mean, I guess.

You cannot be a leader without at least *some* people getting mad at you. In fact, you cannot accomplish *anything* important in life without having someone get upset with you. By its very nature, leadership will offend or upset a certain percentage of individuals. If your son grows up to care too much about what others think of him or whether he inadvertently upsets someone, he will never accomplish anything significant with his life, including raising exceptional children.

But I guess I should not be surprised. Our culture spends a great amount of energy trying to keep men from using their natural, life-giving passions and aggressions. Combine that with many men's natural hesitancy to face confrontation, and you have an entire gender that sits on the sidelines with their hands in their pockets and heads downcast, avoiding any kind of unpleasantness. Of course unpleasantness is a fact of life. Men who do not have courage cannot (or will not) stand up for what is right. And so, for instance, when these men have teenage daughters who rebel in an effort to test their father's love for them, they choose instead to acquiesce and allow their daughters to make life-destroying choices.

Psychologist Michael Gurian comments on the attitude of our culture (especially within the social sciences) toward males and the messages we are sending them: "[The] psychological dialogue regarding 'the changing male role' is laden with minefields regarding how males must become more 'sensitive about feelings' and 'do what women want' and in that minefield are signs well displayed everywhere, signs that read something like: 'Men no longer need to provide and protect. That's traditional male role stuff. Men are needed for something else—though we're not sure what it is. It definitely involves being sensitive and nice, though.'"[6]

The truth is, men *are* still needed to protect women and children from the dangers of the world. Gender politics aside, boys instinctively know that part of their role as men will be to protect and provide for their families, despite what our misguided culture may tell them.

It's not that being nice is bad. Men should be nice, polite, kind, compassionate, empathetic, and understanding as often as possible. But when men are *only* nice, they live shallow, frustrating, and unfulfilling lives—as do those around them. To accomplish anything of significance in life requires us to offend at least some people. Men who are *only* nice are not willing to offend anyone— they never take a stand. A man can have many attributes that can make him successful in life. But if niceness is the most dominant character trait he has, he is probably not someone who can be depended upon to be a strong leader.

I know several very nice young men who are struggling with lust, faith, relationships, careers, and a variety of other issues. We talk about them and I give them some strategies and new perspectives on how to deal with these issues, but the truth is that all men deal with these struggles. I think at some point it becomes a matter of courage (or lack thereof). Are you struggling with lust? Well, welcome to the club—all men struggle with lust. Don't mope around about it. Get some stones and deal with it. Good men struggle with sin and vice just as much as bad men—they just have the courage to deal with it in a productive manner. Don't sit around analyzing it to death. Lack of courage causes us to become paralyzed and not take the action needed to solve problems. I tell these young men to stiffen their spines. There are three billion men on the planet and almost all of them deal with the same issues, especially lust. Some deal with it productively because they love their wives and children; others deal with it by engaging in prostitution, viewing pornography, or having affairs. Which kind of man do you want your son to be?

How to Teach Your Son Courage

> A nation or civilization that continues to produce soft-minded men purchases its own spiritual death on the installment plan.
>
> —Martin Luther King Jr.

The need to take risks in order to feel alive, to do the impossible, to face one's fears and not back down is present in the warrior heart of every boy and man. But too often our culture teaches boys that this drive is bad or unnatural. We punish boys for being too aggressive, too boisterous, and too loud. We medicate them in school when they exhibit normal behaviors that are biologically driven.

Too many young (and old) men today are afraid to be the kind of men they want to be or were created to be because they are fearful of being criticized by a woman or a feminized man (usually sitting behind a news desk or teaching at a university). Since being mocked (especially by a woman) is one of a male's greatest fears, he avoids this at all costs. He alters his behavior to minimize the potential for conflict and criticism. But a man who allows a woman to dictate to him what it means to be a man is all the less a man. Radical feminism has criticized and demonized most masculine behaviors without supplying any better alternatives except to be more like a woman. The truth is, masculinity bestows masculinity—femininity cannot.

Women are generally very poor judges of authentic masculinity. Lately, women seem to have chosen softer, more passive, less aggressive males to mate with, breeding those traits into their boys and making other men aspire to those virtues in order to get sexual fulfillment. This is partially due to a woman's natural inclination to usurp a man's leadership role (see Gen. 3), but also the result of several generations of feminist propaganda that has led many women to believe they *should* be the absolute leaders of their families and homes—even if they cannot consciously articulate that belief. So the woman seeks out and marries a "girlfriend" instead of a strong male presence who would challenge her authority and autonomy. Then she spends her life with a low-grade "fever" of discontentment, complaining she is dissatisfied and unhappy with her life. She insists that her husband take a leadership role, but then criticizes him if he does not lead as she thinks fit.

Lest some of you accuse me of being misogynistic or chauvinistic, I'm not talking about masculine domination. I'm referring to men using the God-given power they have to lift up those under their provision and protection to enable them to live lives greater than would be possible without their healthy masculine influence. To use that power takes courage.

So how do we teach our boys to have courage? First, teach your son to embrace failure. Fear of failure keeps most men from even attempting something. Most males feel humiliated by failure or inadequacy. But males learn best by trial and error; by attempting something, failing, and then persevering until they succeed. Boys who avoid anything they are not sure to succeed at live very limiting lives. No one wins every time. But the only way you always lose is to not try at all.

Developing courage is usually a progressive endeavor. Unless we are faced with circumstances that force us to be courageous (life-or-death situations), it generally takes self-confidence and experience to become courageous. It often takes other males standing beside us (men seldom go to war by themselves). Hence if we can present opportunities to our sons to help them to succeed step by step and become confident, they will likely develop courage on their own. Start with small challenges and work your way up.

Here's a good way to *not* teach your son courage. The first time I decided to play catch with my son, Frank, he was about three years old (probably a little too young). I bought him a little mitt, showed him how to use it, and went out with him to the backyard. At that time in my life, I was a hard-nosed, "sink or swim" kind of guy. I just naturally figured if you learned a skill under the most difficult circumstances, you would be all the better when you tried it under normal conditions. I'm not sure why, but I decided to play catch the first time with a hardball. We stood a couple of feet away from each other and I very gently lobbed it underhanded to him. Of course it hit him square in the mug, causing him to throw down his glove and run into the house, crying for his mother. Frank never much took to baseball after that. Oh, he was a pretty fair little ballplayer through Little League, but he always seemed a bit afraid of the ball.

Modeling courage to our sons requires us to be courageous. Many times as men we avoid things that are unpleasant. In reality we are often afraid to do them and use our veto power as a form of cowardice. We justify not standing up and speaking our mind at school board meetings because we "don't like to speak in public," when in reality we are afraid someone might criticize us. We choose not to have a heart-to-heart conversation with our daughter's date because we don't want to seem un-cool or old-fashioned, when truthfully we are just afraid of confrontation.

We do not address issues in our relationship with our wives until they have become nearly irreparable problems because we fear emotional confrontation and self-examination. Our sons (and daughters) eventually see through this guise and come to believe that if Dad doesn't think anything is important enough to "put it all on the line," then why should they. We teach them to become cowards without even realizing it.

I can remember as a boy seeing several incidents that taught me about courage. I saw these acted out by people around me and observed them on television or in the movies. However, it took some time for those lessons to stick. I think if someone had spoken into my life *along with* that modeling, it would have been so much more effective. We can't brag about our own actions, only model them for our sons. But this is where a spouse, working together as a team, comes in handy. For instance, it would be really difficult and probably unproductive to tell our sons, "Hey, did you see how brave I was there?" But a father could say to his son, "Did you see your mom help that elderly person in the store? I've always appreciated how much courage your mom has that she can walk up to strangers and offer to help them. I'm usually a bit nervous that I'll embarrass myself somehow." Or a mother can say, "Did you notice how your dad always tells young men in public to watch their language because women and children are present? Don't you think that takes courage? That's the kind of bravery that all men should show." Look for opportunities to edify your spouse when they show courage, and always point those times out to your children. Tell your spouse in front of your son how proud you are of them for the courageous action they engaged in. That engrains in your son's psyche the value of acting courageously. He will grow up just naturally assuming that courage is a character trait that all people exhibit.

Your role in life is to shepherd your son into manhood. Shepherds do not produce sheep—sheep produce sheep. Shepherds produce other shepherds. Being a shepherd requires you to have courage in order to protect your flock. Too many people in the church and in our country today are "sheeple"—those who voluntarily acquiesce to suggestions without critical analysis or research. They then lose their individuality and willingly give up their rights.[7] They go along with just about anything as long as it doesn't upset their little world or cause them to have to think too hard or make any difficult choices.

Be a shepherd for your son. Have courage in all you do. Don't condemn him to a life as a cowardly sheeple.

2

Honor and Nobility

Robert E. Lee

*So help me, all it takes for the world to crumble to noth-
ing is for women to lose their virtue and men their honor.*
—Andrew Klavan, *The Identity Man*

THE WORD *honor* MEANS TO BE HONEST, TO BE FAIR,
and to have integrity in one's beliefs and actions with a high
level of respect for ourselves and others. It is an adherence
to what is intrinsically *right*. Honor also entails having a nobleness
of mind, character, or spirit—an exalted moral excellence, if you
will. A man of honor is loyal, faithful, and true to his word. He
keeps his promises and fulfills his duties.

Our culture and the definition of honor have changed over the
generations. Honor used to reflect a man's outer image—the way
he acted and how he conducted himself publicly. Now it is more
about whether a man has inner qualities such as integrity, honesty,
and loyalty.

With these changes, the definition of manhood has changed as
well. Masculinity was highly valued until a few generations ago.

Prior to then, civilizations considered a man to be valued and encouraged men to be as honorable and excellent as possible. The ancient Greeks believed a man should be the best man he could possibly be—to live a life of excellence. The Latin word for manliness or masculine strength is *virtus* (from which we derive the word *virtue*). The Romans too believed in the ideal of *virtus* in association with manliness. They believed a man should live a life of virtue, centered on the traits of valor, courage, fortitude, industriousness, and duty.[1]

Our culture today tends to define manhood as being the opposite of womanhood. But a better definition might be that manhood is the opposite of childhood or, better still, boyhood. For instance, a child is self-centered, fearful, and dependent. A man is (or should be) bold, courageous, respectful, independent, and one who serves others.[2]

One of the results of these changes has been that honor is no longer a valued character trait. Actually, it is in word but not in deed. We talk a lot about honor but seldom see it in action or praise it when we see it acted out. Perhaps this is because it runs contrary to our "age of the individual." Honor requires us to put the needs of others ahead of our own. It requires that we place more value on others than on ourselves. Honor is the heart of authentic masculinity. It differentiates good men from bad men, leaders from loafers. It is the trait that inspires men to accomplish great deeds and make huge sacrifices for the benefit of others. Honor fuels healthy civilization.

Let's look at why honor is important even today (*especially* today) and how to instill it in our sons. Probably all great men throughout history have had honor, but perhaps none are more known for it than General Robert E. Lee.

Robert E. Lee—A Gentleman of Honor

Robert Edward Lee (1807–1870) was a career military officer who commanded the Confederate Army of Northern Virginia in the

American Civil War. Lee is considered one of the greatest generals and military tacticians of all history. He inspired great love and loyalty in the men who followed him. After the Civil War was over, he was admired by his friends and former foes alike as he sought to reconcile the country.

Lee was the son of US Revolutionary War hero Henry "Light Horse Harry" Lee III and graduated second in his class at the United States Military Academy at West Point without a single demerit his entire academic career. Lee's family was one of Virginia's first families, from England in the early 1600s. After being in debtors prison and beaten nearly to death defending the editor of an anti-war newspaper, Harry Lee left the family when Robert was age five, and Lee and his five siblings were raised by his mother with help from relatives. Harry died when young Robert was eleven years old. Lee later married Mary Custis, great-granddaughter of Martha Washington (George Washington's wife). Lee's property, which was seized by the Union army during the Civil War, eventually became Arlington National Cemetery. George Washington (although long dead) was a mentor figure that Lee looked up to throughout his life.[3]

Lee was by all accounts a dedicated father to his children and grandfather to his grandchildren. He enjoyed spending what time he could with his children and later their children, most often engaging in "tickling" matches. Some of the character traits he was widely known for include self-discipline, hard work, modesty, respect, honor, and loyalty.

Lee distinguished himself as an exceptional officer and combat engineer in the United States Army for thirty-two years. During the Mexican War, Lee served under General Winfield Scott. Lee spent days on his own in arduous reconnaissance efforts scouting enemy territory in order to discover the best ways to attack the enemy. After one of these harrowing adventures, Scott declared Lee's performance during the war "the greatest feat of physical and moral courage performed by an individual in my knowledge."

Scott later told President Abraham Lincoln that Lee was worth fifty thousand soldiers to the South.[4]

When Virginia seceded from the Union in April 1861, Lee chose to follow his home state, despite his personal desire for the Union to stay intact and despite the fact that President Abraham Lincoln had offered Lee command of the Union army. Lee felt that loyalty to Virginia and protecting his home and family superseded his personal desires. Many of his peers tried to get him to change his mind, but Lee stayed loyal to his convictions.

During the Civil War Lee quickly rose to become commander of the Confederate army and a close advisor to President Jefferson Davis. Due to his loyalty and concern for them, Lee was beloved by his men and was worshipfully referred to as "Marse [master] Robert" and "Old Bobbie Lee" or, even more respectfully, "The Old Man" by his troops. He was known by his foes simply as "The Grey Fox." Lee inspired his troops like few leaders of men have throughout history. Lee's troops often fought barefoot and hungry, without supplies or reinforcements, yet dominated most of the battles throughout the war.

Lee took pains to avoid civilian casualties, choosing not to involve women and children as many of his Union counterparts did. For example, when Lee led the arrest and capture of John Brown at Harper's Ferry, he specifically ordered the US Marines under his command to break in with sledgehammers and use only bayonets (not the rifles) to overpower the band of violent abolitionists. He ordered the marines to unload their weapons so that none of Brown's civilian hostages might risk injury.[5] Later Lee always made his troops pay for any food or supplies they obtained from civilians, whether fighting in Northern or Southern states.

Despite being greatly outnumbered in men, supplies, and resources, Lee took an undisciplined rabble—basically an armed mob—and turned them into one of the most famous and effective armies in military history. Especially at the beginning of the war he won many battles against significantly greater forces through his audaciously daring and aggressive tactics. He developed young leaders such as Andrew "Stonewall" Jackson and Jeb Stuart, who in turn gained fame under his tutelage. In fact, history might have been different had Lee not been betrayed by having battle plans fall into the hands of his enemies and suffering the loss of his best weapon—General Stonewall Jackson. As commander of the Confederate States army, Lee defeated no less than five of his Union General counterparts before the north finally put General Grant in charge, a man who brutally used his significant advantages in men and supplies to finally overwhelm Lee's forces.

A number of stories speak to the kind of man Robert E. Lee was. While serving as Superintendent of the United States Military Academy, Lee overheard a recalcitrant student contending for what he thought were his rights as a man. General Lee was heard to respond: "Obedience to lawful authority is the foundation of manly character."[6]

Benjamin Harvey Hill Jr. described Lee as

a foe without hate; a friend without treachery; a soldier without cruelty; a victor without oppression, and a victim without murmuring. He was a public officer without vices; a private citizen without wrong; a neighbour without reproach; a Christian without hypocrisy, and a man without guile. He was a Caesar, without his ambition; Frederick, without his tyranny; Napoleon, without his selfishness, and Washington, without his reward.[7]

Another time, General Lee was on his way to Richmond, seated in the extreme end of a railroad car, every seat of which was occupied. At one of the stations, an aged woman of humble appearance entered the car, carrying a large basket. She walked the length of the aisle and not a man offered her a seat. When she was opposite General Lee's seat, he arose promptly and said, "Madam, take this seat." Instantly a score of men were on their feet, and a chorus of voices said, "General, have my seat."

"No, gentlemen," he replied, "if there was no seat for this old lady, there is no seat for me."

It was not long before the car was almost empty. It was too warm to be comfortable.[8]

Biographies vary on the depth of General Lee's faith, but clearly he was a man of strong Christian conviction. Lee stated in letters that he prayed daily for his family and friends, and reportedly prayed with his men during battles. He kept a prayer journal throughout much of his adult life and lived his life by biblical principles.

One of Lee's biographies says of him, "By his achievements, Lee won a high place amongst the great generals of history. Though hampered by lack of materials and by political necessities, his strategy was always daring, and he never hesitated to take the gravest risks. On the field of battle he was as energetic in attack as he was constant in defense, and his personal influence over the men whom he led was extraordinary. No student of the American Civil War can fail to notice how the influence of Lee dominated the course of the struggle, and his surpassing ability was never more conspicuously shown than in the last hopeless stages of the contest. The personal history of Lee is lost in the history of the great crisis of America's national life; friends and foes alike acknowledged the purity of his motives, the virtues of his private life, his earnest Christianity and the unquestioning loyalty with which he accepted the ruin of his party."[9]

Lee lived his life according to a code of honor and chivalry not seen since. He proved that honor and nobility make a man great, or perhaps men naturally become great when they exhibit these traits to the degree that Lee did.

Why Honor and Nobility Are Important

Perhaps no character trait embodies healthy masculinity more than that of honor (healthy honor—other cultures and religions have forms of honor that may not agree with our version of honor in the West). Honor is the soul of masculinity. It is a code that a man lives by that lifts him above mere mediocrity and survival. It enables him to use the incredible power that God has endowed him with to lift the lives of others beyond what they could ever be without his broad shoulders to stand upon. Honor allows a man to stand tall among lesser members of his gender. It inspires him to reject and ignore involvement in self-gratifying activities (like adultery, drugs, lying, or stealing) that sap his ability to live a life of integrity and wholeness. It allows him an opportunity to strive for greatness in life. It motivates him to live his life to a higher standard.

Nobility, then, is the flagstaff of honor. A noble vision gives a man the guidelines by which to live an honorable life. His noble behavior is a sign to the world of the honor he carries within his heart.

Perhaps one of the most profound statements about honor and nobility of all time was this one made by C. S. Lewis. While discussing the desire or propensity of modern society to remove the heart (honor, passion, and noble strength) from the young men of our culture, he predicted, "We continue to clamour for those very qualities we are rendering impossible. . . . In sort of a ghastly simplicity we remove the organ and demand the function. We make men without chests and expect of them virtue and enterprise. We laugh at honour and are shocked to find traitors in our midst. We castrate and bid the geldings be fruitful."[10] The very thing we crave and need most in men today is the very thing we mock and breed out of our young men.

Lewis's prophetic work (written in the 1940s) has come to fruition as social and moral relativism has been adopted by modern thought—in religion, education, and government—opening the door to the post-modern claim that people are free to create their own reality through a sheer act of the will.[11]

Boys without passion become men without passion. Men without passion are like automatons or androids—robots trapped in human skin. Men without passion seldom lead noble or honorable lives. They are apathetic; unable or unwilling to lead their families and communities.

How to Teach Your Son Honor and Nobility

Honorable men and honorable expectations teach boys to become honorable. Being surrounded by men of honor and immersed in an environment steeped in an honor code integrates this trait into a boy's heart. Teach your son what you believe to be important in life. Develop a core set of beliefs that as a family you believe to be foundational and unbreakable. Develop an honor code for your family.

Several honor codes for men worth noting are the West Point Cadet Code that simply put says, "A cadet will not lie, cheat, steal or tolerate those who do." That simple statement in and of itself might be the best philosophy we can teach our young men. The Boy Scout Oath and Law are also pledges worth knowing. (I can still recite them both from memory.)

Set high standards for your son! Boys frequently live up to (or down to) the expectations placed upon them. He who aims for little will accomplish little. Expect great things from him and encourage him to attempt great things. He will never be perfect, but he'll get closer to it if that's his aim. There's an old proverb that says, "He who aims at the sun, will not reach it, to be sure, but his arrow will fly higher than if he aims at an object on a level with himself." When life knocks him down, he has to get back up again. Allow him to fail (because he will) and then encourage him to get back up when he does.

Encourage him to study the lives of great men. Why model yourself after mediocrity? Would you rather he look up to someone like Martin Luther King Jr. or a modern rap artist? Help him to understand that the people he associates with are what he will become. If he wants to be healthy, happy, and successful in life, he needs to hang around people who are healthy, happy, and successful in life.

The Boy Scout Oath

The Oath:

On my honor, I will do my best

To do my duty to God and my country and to obey the Scout Law;

To help other people at all times;

To keep myself physically strong, mentally awake and morally straight.

The Law:

A scout is trustworthy, loyal, helpful, friendly, courteous, kind, obedient, cheerful, thrifty, brave, clean, and reverent.

Teach your son that he doesn't have to be ashamed of being a male. So much of our culture's messages are subliminal or even overt communications that are either unhealthy for males (stereotypes of aggressive thugs or womanizers) or speak the message that males are not good—that being a male is somehow bad just by virtue of his gender. (Men in TV sitcoms are almost universally portrayed as bumbling buffoons.) Some factions of our culture even refer to boys as having "testosterone poisoning." Teach your son that God created man in his image and gave him the power to influence lives for hundreds of years just by what he does or doesn't do with that power. Tell him he matters—that as a man, a husband, and a father he matters more than he will ever know. As a father he will be nearly irreplaceable in the lives of his children—they suffer mightily in his absence. Teach him that people he doesn't even know are constantly watching him to see how a man thinks, acts, solves problems, and faces life.

Next, as a mother and father, determine what social injustices are important to you. Then get involved to make a difference in those areas. Have your sons (and daughters) be a part of that. Help them experience what it is like to actively be a part of trying to make a difference in the world. Help them see you devoting your time to something that matters. Let them see the changes your efforts make in the lives of other people. This can be as simple as financially supporting starving children in other countries. Or as complex as volunteering at soup kitchens, tutoring people who can't read, or demonstrating for a cause you believe in. Though my wife and I are far from hippie protestors, while they were growing up our kids did get dragged along to worthy activities like participating in candlelight prayer vigils at abortion clinics, serving at homeless shelters, helping out at facilities that train kids with special needs or have physical handicaps, and working at our single moms family camps. I believe this helped them realize that there are more important things in life than just themselves. These experiences helped them recognize the nobility of helping others with no expectations in return and the honor that comes from living a life of service for something bigger than just ourselves. Today my daughter is passionate about working with kids with special needs, and my son is a dedicated husband and excited father-to-be.

And finally, another way to instill honor in boys is to teach them manners, or even better, chivalry. Chivalry embodies the traits of honor, dignity, sacrifice, and nobility. These traits are all but forgotten in our culture today, at least on an individual basis. But some organizations such as police, fire, and EMTs, as well as the military, encourage men to exhibit some or all of the described traits, serving the needs of others above their own desires and living by a type of honor code. But as a culture we appear to have devalued these traits to the point that men and boys no longer aspire to them, or possibly don't even know they exist. If anything, young men today are taught to despise authority and use their power for their own self-gratification above all else.

Chivalry seems to be dead today, or as my editor once put it, "has been stomped to death." She has a valid point—you don't see many examples of chivalry today. Frankly, most young men today are not forced to earn the affections of young women—much to the girls' detriment. They are not required to be noble and honorable in any area of life. But if you want your son to marry well and be successful in life, teaching him the art of chivalry will be to his advantage.

Chivalry is more than just manners—it is a way of life. The way a boy or man conducts himself day to day speaks volumes about his character. As a male it takes a conscious effort for me to even consider meeting someone else's needs. It is not an instinctive, reflexive action like it appears to be with most females. Females appear to be wired to either desire to or to just instinctively meet others' needs without much forethought (or probably they are just much more considerate than the average male). But as a male, I am not wired to do this. It's not that I am intentionally selfish; I am just programmed to think about my own needs the majority of the time. I have to consciously think about meeting someone else's needs or I will unconsciously spend most of my energy seeking to meet my own needs. Meeting another's needs is an internal decision that requires intentionality—it doesn't just happen.

For instance, my wife is coming home from Bible study at 9:00 tonight. She just called to ask if I needed anything from the store. She is frequently conscious of what my needs might be. If I were in that same circumstance I would be worrying about getting home and relaxing, not what needs my wife might have. Does that mean I'm selfish? Maybe, but I suspect most males operate on the same level of consciousness and self-focus. If I were stopping at the store anyway I *might* call my wife and ask if she needed something, but it would never dawn on me to go out of my way and make a special stop without being asked.

If that mentality is true for most males (and I believe it is) then it would seem wise to teach them the importance of thinking about the needs of others and not just their own needs.

One of the best ways to instill chivalry in young men is to teach them proper manners and etiquette as boys. Manners are, after all, about respect—respect for oneself and respect for others. Manners teach a boy that he needs to be aware of other people in the world besides himself. So many people appear to be self-focused in our culture today that someone who puts the needs of others ahead of his own stands out like a bright beacon upon a hill. A young man who practices good manners and acts chivalrous has doors opened for him in life that most others do not. Manners lead to respect, which leads to an attitude of understanding that other people are just as or even more important than we ourselves are. This leads to a life of chivalry. Chivalry then leads to living a life of honor and nobility.

There are a number of good resources on teaching boys manners ranging from *The Berenstain Bears Forget Their Manners* to Geoffroi de Charny's *The Book of Chivalry*. But the best way to teach manners is to model them in your home and then hold your son to a high standard in his behavior and treatment of others.

3

Duty

George Washington

What man is a man who does not make the world better?
—*Kingdom of Heaven* (MOVIE),
FROM THE LATIN INSCRIPTION: *Nemo vir*
est qui mundum non reddat meliorem

THE WORD *duty* (FROM THE FRENCH FOR "DUE" AND Latin for "debt") is a term that conveys a moral commitment to someone or something. The moral commitment is one that results in action and is not a matter of passive feeling or mere recognition. When someone recognizes a duty, that person commits himself to the cause involved without considering the self-interested courses of actions that may have been relevant previously. This is not to suggest that living a life of duty precludes one of the best sorts of lives but duty does involve some sacrifice of immediate self-interest.

A duty (in either a moral or legal sense) is an obligatory task, conduct, service, or function that arises from one's position. For instance, someone serving in the military takes an oath to "support and defend the Constitution of the United States against all enemies, foreign and domestic." It is their duty (legal obligation) to serve their country in that capacity if it should be required. Likewise, when a man becomes a father it is his duty (moral obligation) to provide for and protect that child. Oftentimes it is also our civic obligation or duty to serve our fellow man if we are in a position to be best qualified to fulfill that function—even if we are reluctant.

George Washington was such a man.

George Washington—Duty above All Else

> I looked for a man among them who would build up the wall and stand before me in the gap on behalf of the land so I would not have to destroy it, but I found none.
>
> —Ezekiel 22:30 NIV 1984

George Washington (1732–1799) was born on a Virginia tobacco plantation. He could trace his roots back to the first settlers of America. His father died when he was eleven years old, and he went to live with his older brother on the property known as Mount Vernon, which he later inherited. At sixteen he began work as a surveyor and spent the next three years mapping the Virginia wilderness. Young Washington, although an excellent dancer and horseman, was unlucky with the ladies. He was shy and quiet, and it's possible that women might have been afraid of him; while most men in his time stood about five foot five inches tall, Washington was at least six foot two with huge hands and feet. He had reddish brown hair worn in a ponytail and gray-blue, piercing eyes.[1]

Washington was the first president of the United States of America. He led the American victory over Great Britain in the American Revolutionary War as commander-in-chief of the Continental Army from 1775 to 1783 and presided over the writing of the Constitution in 1787. He was the unanimous choice to become the first president of the US (still the only president to garner 100 percent of the electoral votes) and oversaw the creation of a strong, well-financed national government. His leadership style established many forms and rituals of government that have been used since, such as using a cabinet system and delivering an inaugural address. Washington is universally regarded as the "father of his country."

Washington had a vision of a great and powerful nation that would be built along republican lines and using federal power. He sought to use the national government to preserve liberty, improve infrastructure, open the western lands, promote commerce, found a permanent capital, reduce regional tensions, and promote a spirit of American nationalism. Virtually all of the decisions he made, from initially accepting the presidency to limiting his service to two terms (instead of for life), set precedents that are still in force today.

Early in his career, Washington fought with the British in the French and Indian War. In one battle he had two horses shot out from under him, his hat shot off his head, and four musket balls tear through his coat, but he still was not hit![2] He was eventually put in charge of the Virginia regiment and given the task of defending Virginia's frontier. In command of a thousand soldiers, Washington was a disciplinarian who emphasized training. He led his men in brutal campaigns against the Indians in the west, and within ten months various units of his regiment had fought twenty battles and lost a third of their men. Washington's strenuous efforts meant that Virginia's frontier population suffered less than that of other colonies. After the frontier was safe, Washington considered his duty done and went home to marry Martha Custis and settle down as a Virginia planter. Washington was a successful farmer working with different crop rotations and breeding a variety of animals. But British taxation was raising the ire of the American colonies and war loomed on the horizon.

After the Boston Tea Party, England sent troops to occupy Boston and declared English Law in effect. When Paul Revere warned the countryside that the "British are coming!" seventy-seven "minutemen" met the troops in Lexington and the "shot heard round the world" started the Revolutionary War.

In April 1775 after the Battles of Lexington and Concord, the colonies declared war on Great Britain. Washington appeared at the Second Continental Congress in a military uniform, signaling that he was prepared for war. Washington had the military experience, charisma, and bearing of a military leader. He was known as a strong patriot. Virginia, the largest colony, deserved recognition, and New England—where the fighting began—realized it needed Southern support. Washington did not seek the office of commander and even said that he was not equal to it, but there was no serious competition. Congress created the Continental Army on June 14, 1775, and Washington was appointed Major General and commander in chief.

Washington had three tasks during the Revolutionary War. First, he had to lead his men against the British forces. While losing many battles, he never surrendered his army, and, in fact, encouraged them to great feats of courage and endurance. His ability to rally his men and encourage morale helped him hold his bedraggled and dispirited army together during the cold and hungry winter at Valley Forge. Despite being desperately low on men and supplies, his courage and daring earned him the respect of his troops. His brilliantly conceived plan to cross the Delaware River in an icy winter storm and the bloody ensuing march on Christmas night ended in the surprise capture of a Hessian garrison and the city of Trenton, New Jersey.[3]

Second, he was charged with organizing and training an army. His problems with an all-volunteer army included not only lack of gunpowder and supplies but building an army from thirteen separate colonies, which was like recruiting from thirteen different countries. The troops did not like discipline and following orders, and they didn't trust men from other colonies. Once, a snowball fight started between men from different militias. Soon over a thousand soldiers were punching and kicking one another. In one of his few displays of temper, Washington charged on horseback into the middle of the fray, leaped down, and grabbed two soldiers by their collars and lifted them off the ground—one in each hand—and roared commands at the others. The fight ended within seconds.[4]

Third, and most important, Washington embodied armed resistance to the Crown—the man representative of the revolution. His enormous stature and political skills kept congress, the army, the French, the militias, and the states all pointed toward a common goal. After victory had been finalized in 1783, Washington resigned rather than seize power, proving his opposition to dictatorship and his commitment to American republicanism.

Washington's insight into human nature also won him admiration. During the occupation of New Jersey by the British, many colonists had sworn an oath of loyalty to the British. After Washington liberated the state, many of his officers wanted to "punish" these traitors. But Washington knew many had claimed loyalty only because they were afraid. So instead of punishing them he gave them an opportunity to pledge allegiance to the United States. Those who refused were allowed to march unharmed across enemy lines. Washington knew the fastest way to turn a Tory into an American patriot was to send him to British-controlled territory because the Redcoats treated colonists poorly. Given a choice between Washington's kindness and the spite of the British military, many decided to become patriots.[5]

Washington had unusually great physical strength. Thomas Jefferson called Washington "the best horseman of his age," and both American and European observers praised his riding. His favorite hobby was hunting. He did not wear a wig, but powdered his hair. He also suffered from bad teeth his entire life, which caused him great pain. (Historians believe you can see that pain etched on his face on the one-dollar bill.) Contrary to popular lore, he did not wear wooden teeth but dentures made from, among other things, hippo ivory. Many of the stories about his childhood such as throwing a silver dollar across the Potomac River and admitting to chopping down his father's cherry tree ("I cannot tell a lie") are probably not true.

Washington was primarily affiliated with the Anglican and, later, the Episcopalian Church. Eyewitness accounts exist of Washington engaging in private devotions, and he frequently accompanied his wife to church services. Washington avoided the word *God* and instead used the term "Providence." He credited every single victory in war, the miracle of the Constitutional Convention, and the creation of the federal government and the prosperity of the early republic to Providence.

Washington died at home after becoming sick with a cold. The last words in his diary were, "'Tis well." All over the world, men and women were deeply saddened by Washington's death. Napoleon ordered ten days of mourning throughout France. In the United States, thousands wore mourning clothes for months. His remains were moved on October 7, 1837, to the new tomb constructed at Mount Vernon. After the ceremony, the inner vault's door was closed and the key was thrown into the Potomac. Washington is consistently ranked among the top three presidents of the United States, according to polls of both scholars and the general public.

Why Duty Is Important

> Duty is mine; consequences are God's.
>
> —General T. J. "Stonewall" Jackson

Duty requires us to do things that need to be done whether or not we want to do them. Many boys I know want to become men because they believe they can do whatever they want once they become an adult. The truth is, though, that the very definition of a man is one who doesn't do some things he does want to do and does some things he doesn't want to do because that benefits those who are under his leadership and charge. George Washington knew that his duty to his country took precedence over his personal desires.

In the past, men had a sense of pride in fulfilling what were considered their natural responsibilities and duties. Chief among these were their natural roles as guide, protector, and provider. Those duties were a man's responsibility alone, and he did not lean on his wife or children, nor expect society to support him. When burdens became heavy, he did not run away or turn to others. He looked to himself for solutions, reorganizing his life, reevaluating his situation, and possibly eliminating unnecessary obligations. These roles were accomplished through the feeling of personal fulfillment and satisfaction he received (1) from proving his worth—reaching objectives, overcoming obstacles, and exercising his unique talents and abilities, (2) by making a worthy contribution to society, and (3) with character development—becoming a more worthy person.

This mentality is healthy for a young male for a number of reasons. He derives a great sense of self-esteem and self-confidence by being self-sufficient and fulfilling his roles as provider and protector. Overcoming obstacles and solving problems develop character and refine his spirit. As a man works patiently and diligently to provide comforts for his family he quickly learns to become unselfish. Marriage is one of the greatest tools for personal development for a young male, especially regarding his duties. It provides incentives unknown to him before marriage.[6]

It would seem now, though, that the industrialized nations have quietly but quite completely moved into a new paradigm for how society is supposed to function. This means that the foundational ethos that had been the fabric of the Christian-Judeo societies has been displaced, particularly as it applies to males.

This former ethos could be reduced to the simple belief that *some things are more important than the individual.* This is what duty is all about—making sacrifices for something more important than we are.

Such tenets of duty might include (1) sacrificing self for the welfare of others, (2) being honorable or honest even if it costs you, (3) maintaining/protecting the sanctity of marriage and family, (4) protecting the dignity/image of foundational societal institutions such as the legal system, government, or school authorities, and (5) being accountable to a higher power (Creator) even when you don't want to be.

For the seventeenth through twentieth centuries, this underlying belief system (primarily based on the Ten Commandments) was generally accepted by our societies. This acceptance existed either willingly, grudgingly, or perhaps even in active rebellion against the concepts. But almost all people acknowledged there was this basic system of beliefs that was the foundation for any discussion on people's actions.

The twenty-first century has now pushed aside this previous system of beliefs. In its place, it has almost completely installed a new ethos. This ethos has ushered in a new belief system consisting of postmodernism, morally and truthfully relativistic with an entitlement attitude. This new underlying belief can be reduced to this: *There is nothing that is more important than the individual.*

The irony of this new ethos is that if nothing is more important than the individual, then the individuals living in such a milieu have been cast adrift into a lonely existence of *unimportance.* This follows because, first, if there are no superior institutions (besides government) to give order, stability, and protection, then each individual is completely on their own and, ultimately, helpless against whatever forces might come against them. And, second, if nothing is more important than the individual, then the individual is *alone.* All other people are separate, of less importance, and thus helpless for emotionally bonding with the individual.

Men are no longer universally looked to for leadership in our society or to fulfill their primary duties though God has given and equipped them with the duty to provide leadership in at least three key areas (spiritual teaching would be a fourth):

Provision: Men are no longer necessarily the providers in their families. Women quite often earn as much or more than their husbands. Also, an ever-increasing number of men are unable to find employment or are becoming greatly underemployed, without the ability to earn enough to support their families.

Protection: The natural aggressiveness in males that is so important for offering protection is being suppressed. Schools starting with kindergarten on up through high school are condemning normal male obstreperousness. Consider how many boys are being placed on medications to calm them or keep them from being disruptive. Soldiers are condemned for not being properly gracious and gentle in the midst of battle. Even professional football athletes are having rules enforced and massive fines imposed to cut out aggressiveness on the field and major league baseball pitchers can't throw a pitch even remotely close to being inside or high and tight without evoking a reprimand from the umpire. If he continues to pitch inside he will be ejected from the game.

Leadership: Many men are no longer actually occupying the position of being the leaders in families. Women have steadily been freed from previous barriers, raised up in their capabilities, and installed in positions of authority and leadership. Currently enrollment in college is about 60 percent women and 40 percent men. As this naturally plays out in our society, women will increasingly occupy positions of power.[7]

Duty today is considered old-fashioned, archaic, and even irrelevant. And yet our culture suffers because men do not live lives of duty—they do not sacrifice themselves for the benefit of others in either public or private arenas. When men do not live lives of duty, we see politicians who use their positions for self-gain instead of the benefit of all. We see fatherless children and single mothers who suffer mightily because men would rather seek personal fulfillment than sacrifice for the good of their families.

George Washington lived a life of duty. All he wanted to be was a land-owning country gentleman. He did not feel qualified to be commander in chief of the Army during the war but felt compelled to accept that role as the most experienced and qualified man for the position. After the war he did not want to oversee the revision of the Articles of Confederation and creation of a constitution but felt compelled when convinced that his presence was necessary. Finally, he reportedly did not want to serve as president but knew it was his duty because the Constitution might not be ratified if he did not fulfill the position. Our country would not be here today if not for his willingness to fulfill his duty as a man.

How to Teach Your Son Duty

It is impossible to rightly govern a nation without God and the Bible.

—George Washington

Teach your son that as a man he has the great power to impact and influence lives. In fact, even as a boy, other people (usually younger boys) are looking up to him and watching him as a role model—generally people he doesn't even know about. Sometimes hundreds or thousands of people's lives are impacted by the things we do or don't do or even the things we say or don't say. Fathers especially have the ability to touch the lives of people for generations. The lives of people they don't know and will never meet are being impacted by the choices and decisions they make today. Your son needs to know about that power so he can learn to use it responsibly. He needs to know that he has a duty to use that power to the best of his ability.

One of the things I am most excited about and proud of happened in the spring of 2010 in the US Virgin Islands (USVI). A sixty-two-year-old grandmother and former senator from the islands had read my book, *Better Dads, Stronger Sons*, at an airport during a business trip. She was impressed enough to buy ten copies to give to business and government leaders back home and ask them to help sponsor me for a weeklong speaking tour of the islands. (Tough duty, I know, but someone has to suffer through this kind of work.) Reportedly, the USVI has a very high fatherless rate, and they were seeing more and more violence among the young men there—especially during the annual Carnival, a monthlong celebration on the islands.

They brought me in just before Carnival to speak across the islands with the message that men, and especially fathers, are important. To facilitate that message, all of my speaking events were either recorded and/or broadcast live by between one to three radio stations. Apparently, the USVI is a very radio-friendly culture with most people listening to talk radio. Because of this experience, I made connections with several radio stations and their show hosts. The one venue where I spoke without a broadcast was at the state penitentiary. While speaking to the men there I emphasized how important they were and that their lives had value and meaning. I told them how much the young people of the islands looked up to them. Afterward, the men wanted to know what they might be able to do to make a difference in the world—after all they were imprisoned. An idea formed. What if the men were to record public service announcements (PSAs) for the radio stations, telling young people that violence and crime are not glamorous and that being incarcerated is not an honorable way to live life? That would be using their influence and power as men in a noble manner! We quickly connected the men with a radio station and the PSAs were recorded and broadcast just before Carnival time.

I can't say whether or not those PSAs made a difference in the rate of violence during Carnival, although I heard anecdotal evidence that they did. I do know that at least some men who formerly believed their lives were of no value now know they can make a difference in the world. And if only one young person was kept from going to prison or had their life spared because of one of those messages, then the effort was worth it.

Help your son to learn that everyone can do something to make the world a better place. It doesn't matter how old you are, how young you are, or how many mistakes you've made. God has a plan for your life and wants to use you to impact the world. Your son's duty is to make his best effort to find out God's plan for his life and then fulfill his role.

Investing in family and relationships also teaches boys about duty. A boy learns about his duty as a father and husband by what is modeled to him by his parents. Since we generally spend the most time on things we truly believe are the most important in life, this means we have to make sacrifices to spend time together. If Dad and Mom model an example of investing in family and friends, then that will be passed along.

Next, you can help your son learn about duty by teaching him the value of delayed gratification. Delayed gratification is a concept that is almost nonexistent in our culture today. With the availability of easy credit, almost no one waits and saves enough money to pay cash for anything today. No one has to wait for more than two minutes for their food order, and with email, text messaging, and cell phones no one has to wait to communicate instantly with anyone on the planet. With overnight (sometimes same day) delivery service no one has to wait for snail mail to receive whatever they want to buy.

Delayed gratification seems like a strange way to teach someone duty, but duty is all about putting aside our wants and needs for the benefit of others. Those who have learned the value of delayed gratification understand the concept of duty at a deeper level. They understand why it is necessary and what benefits come from it. Through the lesson of delayed gratification, they appreciate what they receive more. For instance, waiting to have sexual intercourse until you are married helps you appreciate it so very much more than engaging in it from the time you first meet. Having to save up and pay cash for your first car means you will appreciate it more, value it more, and probably take better care of it than if it were given to you.

Most of all, delayed gratification teaches sons to understand that the world does not revolve around them and that some things are more important than their wants and needs. Each of us must fulfill duties during our lifetime. As husbands and fathers we have duties to our wives and children to provide for them and protect them—whether or not we feel like it! Some men become involved in the military and have a duty to protect our country—sometimes at great cost of life or limb. Without their sacrifices the freedoms each of us enjoys would be nonexistent.

Duty matters—without it neither individuals nor cultures can attain greatness.

4

Integrity and Loyalty

John Wooden

Integrity without knowledge is weak and useless, and knowledge without integrity is dangerous and dreadful.
—Samuel Johnson

I have prepared for death all of my life by the life I lived.
—Socrates

INTEGRITY IS THE ADHERENCE TO MORAL AND ETHICAL principles. It is often (although not always) described as a soundness of moral character. Honesty is generally one of the traits attributed to integrity. Integrity encompasses an entire lifestyle or worldview—it is a wholeness of character. It is the consistency of actions, values, principles, and expectations in a man's life that determine the level of his integrity. Integrity is the opposite of hypocrisy.

Loyalty on the other hand is the faithfulness to commitments or obligations. It is a feeling or attitude of devoted attachment and affection. It is also faithfulness to a person, group, cause, or country.

No man was more loyal or lived life with more integrity than John Wooden.

John Wooden—Man of Integrity and Loyalty

One of the men I have admired most is the legendary coach of the UCLA Bruins basketball team, Coach John Wooden (1910–2010). It was difficult for me to write this short bio on Coach Wooden because he has played such a huge role in my life as a distant mentor, and I often found myself too close to the subject matter to be objective. I patterned myself as a basketball coach after him and was influenced mightily as a man by his life philosophy.

John Wooden was the first basketball player to be named an All-American three times and won a national championship at Purdue while graduating with academic honors. He then taught high school and coached basketball for several years before taking over as basketball coach at what is now Indiana State University. In 1947, Wooden's basketball team won the Indiana Intercollegiate Conference title and received an invitation to the National Association of Intercollegiate Basketball (NAIB) National Tournament in Kansas City—a huge honor at the time! Wooden, however, refused the invitation, citing the NAIB's policy banning African-American players. One of Wooden's players was Clarence Walker, an African-American. In 1948, Wooden again led Indiana State to the conference title. By then the NAIB had reversed its policy banning African-American players, and Wooden coached his team to the NAIB National Tournament final, losing to Louisville. This was the only championship game a Wooden-coached team ever lost.

Circumstances soon brought him to UCLA as the head coach, and he immediately fashioned an abrupt turnaround to a faltering program. Wooden won 620 games in twenty-seven seasons at UCLA and was named Coach of the Year a total of six times. He was the first person to be inducted into the Basketball Hall of Fame as both a player and a coach.

With his fast-breaking, well-conditioned teams that wore down opponents with a full-court zone press that forever changed the style of college basketball, Coach Wooden (nicknamed the Wizard of Westwood) set a number of records that will probably never be broken, including winning ten NCAA championships over a twelve-year period (seven in a row) and winning eighty-eight straight games during one stretch. His teams won thirty-eight straight NCAA tournament games, and had four perfect seasons.[1]

But perhaps of more importance, Coach Wooden was the epitome of integrity and loyalty his entire life. Beloved and revered by his players, he changed the lives of every young man who played for him through the powerful values and life lessons he taught them—perhaps his greatest gift to his players that each would carry throughout their lives. Kareem Abdul-Jabbar said of him, "He never swore at us and never talked to us about winning. Even while winning all those championships, Coach was much more concerned about having a positive effect on the lives of all the young men who played for him."[2]

He was the master of the simple one- or two-sentence homily, instructive little messages. He taught the team "game" and had only three hard-and-fast rules—no profanity, no tardiness, and no criticizing fellow teammates. Layered beneath that seeming simplicity, though, was a slew of life lessons—primers on everything from how to put on your socks correctly to how to maintain poise. Players were clean-shaven with short hair. Each player learned Wooden's "Pyramid of Success," a chart he used to both inspire players and sum up his personal code for life. Industriousness and enthusiasm were its cornerstones; faith, patience, loyalty, and self-control were some of the building blocks. At the top of the pyramid was competitive greatness.[3]

He believed that a role model was the most powerful form of education and that children needed good models more than

Coach Wooden's Two Sets of Threes

First Set:

Never lie.
Never cheat.
Never steal.

Second Set:

Don't whine.
Don't complain.
Don't make excuses.

critics. Coach Wooden's father was a huge influence in his life. In his book on Coach Wooden's life philosophy, author Pat Williams says this about him and the role of his father: "I have been searching for the wellsprings of this man's greatness as a leader and a human being. I've become convinced that both the greatness and the goodness of John Wooden can be traced to his father."[4] Wooden's admiration for his father inspired him to follow a set of ethics or an honor code that his father developed. It consisted of a set of simple values that provided a compass for the way he lived his life. Former player Andy Hill said, "Coach never talked about that seven-point creed around us. He didn't need to. He *lived* that creed. He *was* that creed. And because he was, his players got those principles without even realizing it. When you truly *live* your creed, you don't have to talk about it."[5]

Wooden was married for fifty-three years to the love of his life, Nellie. Coach Wooden was so dedicated to her that after her death in 1985, he continued to write Nell a love letter every month for the next twenty-five years. He faithfully placed those letters under her pillow on her side of the bed until he passed away in 2010, going to be with his beloved wife.[6]

Coach Wooden was a devout Christian, considering his beliefs more important to him than basketball. "I have always tried to make it clear that basketball is not the ultimate. It is of small importance in comparison to the total life we live. There is only one kind of life that truly wins, and that is the one that places faith in the hands of the Savior."[7]

Coach Wooden's Seven-Point Creed

- Be true to yourself.
- Make each day your masterpiece.
- Help others.
- Drink deeply from good books, especially the Bible.
- Make friendship a fine art.
- Build a shelter against a rainy day.
- Pray for guidance and give thanks for your blessings every day.

His life of integrity and loyalty affected everyone who came in contact with him and millions who didn't. The influence of this humble, caring man positively touched the lives of anyone who brushed against him. His greatest wish upon meeting his Maker would be that God would say, "Well done."

Why Integrity and Loyalty Are Important

Try not to become a man of success but rather try to become a man of value.

—Albert Einstein

Integrity and loyalty are two different traits yet they seem to go together like hand in glove. Integrity (in a moral or ethical context) is a way of living that encompasses our entire lifestyle. It is a worldview in that it seeps into all areas of our life. It's an internal value system we live out on a daily basis that people observe and associate with us. Integrity involves an adherence to moral and ethical principles, honesty, and a soundness of moral character. Integrity is the opposite of hypocrisy. Integrity is regarded as the honesty and truthfulness or accuracy of one's actions. It is acting in private and in public in ways that correspond to our value system without compromising them even when the situation dictates that acting that way is not in our best interest. Given the amount of dishonesty our children are exposed to on a daily basis in the world today, it can be very difficult to teach them the value of honesty and integrity.

Loyalty is equally important as it saturates every fiber of our being. Loyalty means we stick by our spouse and children even when times are difficult (which life always is). It teaches our sons that men are faithful to their vows and to their word.

It takes conscious effort to live a life of integrity because we encounter so many gray areas every day. My friend Tony Rorie of Men of Honor Ministries says the difference between great and mediocre men lies in small compromises.

The Bible speaks about integrity in many places, but the book of Proverbs speaks to it in the most direct fashion. Proverbs 10:9 says, "The man of integrity walks securely, but he who takes crooked paths will be found out" (NIV 1984). Proverbs 11:3 says, "The integrity of the upright guides them, but the unfaithful are destroyed by their duplicity" (NIV 1984). And Proverbs 20:7 says, "The righteous man walks in his integrity; his children are blessed after him" (NKJV).

I frequently encourage people with the principle that doing the right thing for the right reason, even if we fail, is not failure. It is faithfulness. And faithfulness is always rewarded. Not always in the way or timing we would like, but faithfulness *always* gets rewarded. God loves faithfulness. In 1 Samuel 26:23, we read, "The LORD rewards everyone for their righteousness and faithfulness" (NIV).

The benefits of living a life of integrity are many. When we live lives of integrity, we never have to worry about our conscience. Integrity brings us into a closer relationship with God (not to mention our wives and children!). A life of integrity leaves a powerful legacy for our children and grandchildren. People of integrity and loyalty are rare in our culture and so they are noticed and admired. Last, a life of integrity is one that has no regrets.

How to Teach Your Son Integrity and Loyalty

> I thank John Wooden every day for all his selfless gifts, his lessons, his time, his vision, and especially his patience. . . . This is why we call him Coach.
>
> —Bill Walton

Once again, the best way to teach the traits of loyalty and integrity is through our modeling. Does the way we live our life speak those character traits to our children? They know us better than anyone else. No matter what you think you are hiding from your children, they probably know more about it than you think. We might look good on the outside to people in the community, but what are our personal conduct and conversations like in the privacy of our own homes?

What are some examples of integrity (or hypocrisy) that our children could easily be exposed to? Do we keep the money when the store clerk accidentally gives us too much change back from a purchase or do we give it back even when we have to make a special trip because we've already left the premises? Do you skimp on your workout at the gym? (Confession—I do if I'm not with an instructor who pushes me.) Do you cheat on your taxes—even a little? Think your kids don't know if you cheat on your taxes? Think again. Not only do our children know more about what is going on in our private lives than we think they do (it's their job—it's a form of survival), they also see *all* our actions through innocent eyes. This means that actions that are incongruent with our stated philosophy are easily noticed.

The truth is, when you cheat on your taxes (or engage in other forms of dishonesty like little white lies), your behavior is compromised in other areas of life as well—areas you may not even be aware of. When our actions do not match our words our children notice. This is hypocrisy—the opposite of integrity. Kids are experts at spotting and picking up on hypocrisy. How do you treat your spouse? Do you treat him or her with respect or with contempt? How do you act when you are under pressure situations? We can talk all we want about having integrity, but the way we conduct ourselves under stress and pressure reveals what our values really are.

What about loyalty? What does loyalty look like when modeled on an everyday basis? Do we speak highly of our friends (or our spouse) behind their backs, even when they've done something to make us angry? Or do we comment critically on their weaknesses and foibles? Do we defend our spouse even when they've made a mistake? There's a difference between being supportive and loyal versus enabling someone to engage in destructive behaviors. Can your spouse count on your support during times of trouble—even when they are sick, acting ugly, or struggling with life? If you are divorced, do you still show respect for the mother or father of your children even if you disagree with their perspective or lifestyle? There's a difference between respecting someone and condoning their actions. Respecting them as a person does not mean you condone their actions. It does mean that for the best interest of your child you do not impugn their character or take out your anger against that person in ways that are damaging to your child.

Part of living life with integrity is living by a "code" of principles. It means having a value system in place to help make tough decisions. Generally, this code requires us to use principles and not emotions to make decisions. Emotions are too easily manipulated and often end in well-intentioned but ill-advised choices.

Suppose two star players on a basketball team break curfew the night before they are to play in the state championship game. The coach has a longstanding rule that if any players break curfew they will be suspended for the next game. But to enforce that rule will mean the players will not play in the championship game and the team will probably lose. What should the coach do?

As with any decision, a number of consequences can result, impacting many individuals and entities. All of the high school students as well as the entire town are excited about this opportunity. Additionally, the coach and all the players have been waiting for years for this chance and may never get another opportunity like this again. Enforcing the rule could potentially hurt everyone in the community, the school, and on the team. Would a decision like that be fair to them? Should the entire team and town suffer the consequences of the actions of one or two players?

When looking at this decision from an emotional perspective, no, it is not fair for everyone to suffer for the actions of a few. However, several issues are at stake here. Are individuals more important than the team? Should rules (ethics) be enforced according to situations and circumstances instead of as universal principles? Is there such a thing as right and wrong?

One of the most important attributes of sports is that the rules are the same for everyone. No one is more special than another, and thus the playing field is level for everyone. The purpose of sports is not necessarily to win (although that is nice) but to teach young people life skills they will need to be successful for the rest of their lives, such as how to be a team player, a hard worker, respectful, and self-disciplined.

To compromise the rules in this case, while seeming to benefit everyone in the short term, would actually hurt all of them in the long term. It would send the message that the school and the entire town stand for situational ethics and that some people are not subject to the same rules as everyone else. Even though it would probably cost him his job, the coach should enforce the rules and suspend these two players, causing them to miss the state championship game.

In principle, this seems to be an easy decision. But what if you were the coach? Or what if one of the offending players was your son? Would the decision still be so clear cut? It would if you wanted to teach your son the meaning of integrity. This is also how we teach young males to make decisions based on principle and not emotions. This would be a hard-won lesson every young man on that team would remember for the rest of his life.

I have a pastor friend who was unjustly terminated from his position, denied monetary benefits he was entitled to, and had his reputation publicly slandered by the elder board. In his grief he very naturally wanted to share his side of the story to set the record straight, also publicly. He would even have been justified in reporting the church to the labor board to get benefits he had earned. However, I counseled him to take the high ground. We talked about putting the church itself ahead of his own needs and desires. I cautioned him to maintain his integrity as it would be what he remembered most about this incident. I advised him to look at what he could learn from this event that would benefit him in the future. Years later, he remarked that he was glad he had taken the high road—he came away with his self-respect and integrity intact and it means a lot to him today. So often we are programmed to react emotionally—it *feels* so good at the time. But I have found that taking time to think through circumstances and making decisions using principles, and not emotions, serves me much better in life in the long run. Being loyal to myself, my family and friends, and my principles allows me to maintain my integrity and sleep at night despite what might be going on in my life.

The truth is not valued in our culture. In fact, the truth is considered offensive by many (including—maybe *especially*—by many Christians). Truth is the new "hate speech." Instead we value "niceness" above all else. Let's not offend anyone, even if it means lying so that we don't hurt their feelings. In fact the "truth" is considered a crime in some arenas. You can see this illustrated by how outraged the mainstream media is whenever anyone says anything that is an absolute truth. Try to raise a discussion as to whether homosexuality is genetic or environmentally caused and you'll be accused of being a homophobe. Try to have a discussion about a woman's "right" to have an abortion and you'll be smeared with as vitriolic a response as is imaginable. Wonder publicly whether it's a good idea to allow Sharia law to creep into our judicial system and you'll be accused of being an "Islamophobe." Disagree with anyone's opinion about anything and they'll automatically label you a "hater."

But ignoring and avoiding any topic that might cause someone to become upset or uncomfortable, just because political correctness dictates that we do, does not make their view the truth. In fact, not talking about it likely just breeds resentment and even hatred toward the subject being avoided. It *encourages* hate—ignorance always does. When we are not allowed to exercise our First Amendment right of freedom of speech, we aren't an "enlightened" society; we just develop ignorant people.

Always be completely honest with your son. If he asks a question that is out of bounds, tell him why you won't answer but never tell him "little white lies" to protect him. That sets a bad example of situational ethics. In fact, share your own integrity challenges with your son. He needs to know that even you (like everyone) struggle with this issue, but more importantly how you handle it when it arises.

Your son needs truth in his life. He needs to know what you believe to be true. He cannot live his life with integrity if he does not know what he believes. He needs to know what is true even when everyone else says it isn't, and he needs to know what is *not* true even when everyone else believes it is. He needs to learn to look at an issue from all sides; weigh what is credible, logical, and believable; and then make a decision using critical thinking skills to determine what is true and what is false.

Our education system has seemed to make a conscious decision to quit teaching students how to develop and use critical thinking skills. In most of the high school and college classes I have sat through, generally only one side of an issue is presented as the truth. Seldom is a topic looked at objectively without the instructor's bias being used as a yardstick to determine what is good and what is bad. This does an incredible disservice to our young people in that they are then easily swayed in their opinions and decision making by whatever they hear on and see in the media. Life's issues are seldom black and white. The ability to look behind an issue and see the motives, circumstances, agenda, and bigger picture often clarifies the situation beyond what was initially observed. A partial truth is frequently worse than an outright lie. Too often we are taught to allow our emotions, not our principles, to determine what we believe to be true. But emotions are an incredibly poor fulcrum to base our decision making upon. Emotions are easily manipulated and are frequently triggered by unsound beliefs and painful experiences. Principles, however, are based on a concrete foundation of well-thought-out morals and ethics.

A man or boy who knows what he believes can use those principles as a guiding foundation to live a life of integrity and loyalty. And we desperately need loyal men of integrity.

5

Self-Discipline

Theodore Roosevelt

Every man has a latent power within him. Author Sam Keen called this energy our "fire in the belly." Plato called it thumos, or manly spiritedness. Thumos is a man's life force, the engine of soul which inspires bold, courageous action and the pursuit of glory.

—Brett and Kate McKay,
The Art of Manliness Manvotionals: Timeless Wisdom and Advice on Living the 7 Manly Virtues

Self-discipline is the training and control of one-self and one's conduct, such as the act of disciplining or power to discipline one's own feelings or desires. It is the correction or regulation of oneself for the sake of improvement. It is the ability to motivate oneself in spite of a negative emotional state. Qualities often associated with self-discipline include willpower, restraint, hard work, self-control, and persistence.

Self-discipline and willpower go hand in hand. Self-discipline is impossible without the internal strength of willpower. An analogy helps define the relationship between the two: "Where willpower is the muscle, self-discipline is the structured thought that controls that muscle."[1]

One of the men who have exemplified hard work and self-discipline throughout history is Theodore Roosevelt. Roosevelt has been a huge influence in my life, and whenever I am feeling down I read a book about him to get inspired again.

Theodore Roosevelt—Strong as a Bull Moose

Discipline is the soul of an army. It makes small numbers formidable; procures success to the weak, and esteem to all.

—George Washington

Theodore Roosevelt (1858–1919) was the twenty-sixth (and youngest) president of the United States. He was known for his robust personality, range of interests and achievements, and vigorous masculinity. He was a leader of the Republican Party and founder of the short-lived Progressive ("Bull Moose") Party of 1912. Before becoming president, he held offices at the city, state, and federal levels. Roosevelt's achievements as a naturalist, explorer, hunter, author, and soldier are as much a part of his fame as his political accomplishments.

Theodore Roosevelt's father played a huge role in his life. Young Teddy called his father the "best man I ever knew." When Teddy was four, his father began spending long periods of time away from home working with President Lincoln during the Civil War. Biographer Edmund Morris describes what happened to young Roosevelt during his father's absence:

The child was simultaneously sinking into what seemed like chronic invalidism. From the moment his father left home, the catalog of Teedie's [Teddy's] ailments became continuous. He suffered from coughs, colds, nausea, fevers, and a congenital form of nervous diarrhea. . . . On top of all this his asthma was worsening. . . . Lack of appetite brought about symptoms of malnutrition. . . . How much Teedie's asthma was aggravated by the absence of his father may be inferred from some remarks he made thirty-seven years later: "Handsome dandy that he was, the thought of him now and always has been a sense of comfort. I could breath [sic], I could sleep, when he had me in his arms. My father—he got me breath, he got me lungs, strength—life."[2]

But his father did not coddle him—in fact, he pushed him quite strenuously. After being sickly his entire childhood, by age twelve young Roosevelt was tall but puny, frail, skeletal, and physically weak. His father told him, "Theodore, you have the mind but you have not the body, and without the help of the body the mind cannot go as far as it should. You must *make* your body. It is hard drudgery to make one's body, but I know you will do it."[3] Teddy immediately began a strenuous workout regimen that, through rigid self-discipline and determination, eventually built his body into one that became famous as being "as strong as a bull moose."

Roosevelt attended Harvard College, where he studied biology, boxed, rowed, edited a magazine, was the member of several fraternities and clubs, and developed an interest in naval affairs. He had a photographic memory and graduated Phi Beta Kappa with an AB *magna cum laude*. He was a serious historian and authority on hunting, the outdoors, politics, and frontier history. He started Columbia Law School but dropped out after one year to be elected to the New York State Assembly. In 1884 his wife and his mother died on the same day, and he left politics and went to the frontier, becoming a rancher and rough-hewn cowboy in the "Badlands" in the Dakotas. Returning several years later, he ran for mayor and served for some time as the New York City Police Commissioner, where he radically reformed the department from one of the most corrupt to one of integrity.

When the Spanish-American War broke out between the US and Cuba, Roosevelt gained fame when he resigned as Assistant

Secretary of the Navy and formed a voluntary cavalry regiment known as the "Rough Riders." Hand selecting a group of cowboys and hard men from such diverse environs as the Western territories to Ivy League institutions, he formed the first US Volunteer Cavalry Regiment. Under his leadership, the Rough Riders became famous for dual charges up Kettle Hill and San Juan Hill. For the battle of San Juan Hill he was nominated for the Medal of Honor, which was later disapproved—possibly because he made statements in the press about the terrible health conditions troops were exposed to, which embarrassed the White House. In 2001 he was posthumously awarded the medal and remains the only president to have earned the award.

In 1898 he was elected governor of New York and later nominated for vice president on the Republican ticket. In 1901, when President Taft was assassinated, Roosevelt became president at age forty-two. He still remains the youngest president. Roosevelt's foreign policy was to "Speak softly and carry a big stick." He was the driving force behind the completion of the Panama Canal and negotiated an end to the Russo-Japanese War, for which he received the Nobel Peace Prize.

After leaving office in 1909, he engaged in a significant African hunting expedition. He traveled from modern-day Kenya to the Belgian Congo, along the Nile to Khartoum in modern Sudan, hunting specimens (everything from insects to big game) for the Smithsonian Institution and for the American Museum of Natural History in New York.

One event that illustrates his physical toughness happened when he was campaigning for the Bull Moose Party (the short-lived political party he started after breaking from the Republican Party) in 1912. An assassin shot him in the chest, but the bullet first passed through his steel eyeglass case and a thick copy of the speech he was carrying in his jacket. As an experienced hunter and anatomist, Roosevelt correctly concluded that since he was not coughing blood, the bullet had not completely penetrated the chest wall into his lung, and declined suggestions he go to the hospital. Instead, he delivered his scheduled speech with blood seeping into his shirt. Speaking for ninety minutes, his opening comments to the crowd were, "Ladies and gentlemen, I don't know whether you fully understand that I have just been shot, but it takes more than that to kill a Bull Moose." Afterward, x-rays showed that the bullet had traversed three inches of tissue and lodged in Roosevelt's chest muscle but did not penetrate the pleura. Since it was more dangerous to attempt to remove the bullet than to leave it in place, Roosevelt carried it with him for the rest of his life.

Roosevelt later led a major scientific expedition to the Amazon jungles but contracted diseases that, along with the bullet in his chest, ultimately led to his death. He continued to be a force politically and was an enthusiastic supporter of the Boy Scouts of America until his death in 1919. The US vice president at the time, Thomas R. Marshall, said, "Death had to take Roosevelt sleeping, for if he had been awake, there would have been a fight." Roosevelt has consistently been ranked by scholars as one of the greatest US presidents.

Why Self-Discipline Is Important

> In reading the lives of great men, I found that the first victory they won was over themselves . . . self-discipline with all of them came first.
>
> —Harry S. Truman

I have recently been taking acting lessons to try to improve my speaking ability and on-stage presence. If you know me then you know that acting lessons are probably the *last* thing you would ever expect me to be involved in. Emoting in front of other people is way, *way* outside my comfort zone. Frankly accessing and understanding my emotions is difficult, if not downright painful. It takes a great deal of personal self-discipline to continue going to these classes (especially when I have to pay for them), acting in front of others, recording my performance on video, and then having the teacher critique my performance over and over again. But I am finding that in order to help others receive the message God has given me I need to stretch and grow so that I can meet people at *their* point of need and not just in ways I am necessarily comfortable reaching them. I wish it was a lesson I had learned as a parent a long time ago. However, as a benefit to those efforts, I am finding that I am learning more about myself and actually healing in some areas I was wounded. Without the willpower to go through this I would not receive the personal benefits nor would I be better able to touch the audiences I speak in front of.

In one of Plato's works, *Phaedrus*, he uses the symbol of a chariot to explain the interplay between the three factions of a man's soul. The chariot is pulled by two winged horses, one white and one dark colored. The white horse represents a man's *thumos*; strong and willing. The dark one is obstinate, lumbering, and deformed—it represents all of man's bodily appetites. The Charioteer (symbolizing reason and intellect) guides these horses. Together with the white horse he forces the dark horse to fall into line and guides them all toward honorable aims. Without reason and intellect guiding them, the two horses would move in opposite directions or not at all. Plato's point is that only by harnessing one's passions and lusts through self-discipline can we move forward and reach our full potential in life.[4]

Without self-discipline we can never achieve our full potential. You could be a naturally gifted musician or athlete but if you did not have the discipline to practice hard and often, you would never develop your full ability. You could be extremely intelligent, but if you did not study and learn you would waste that ability. We are extremely handicapped if we base our decisions *purely* on our comfort level. If we don't develop the capacity for self-discipline, we deprive ourselves of not only greater likelihood of success but also larger and long-lasting satisfactions.

Without self-discipline we can never accomplish our dreams. I have so many people come up to me and tell me they want to write a book. But almost none of them ever do. Is it because they can't? No—it's because writing a book is hard and they do not have the discipline to sit down and do it. So many people have unfulfilled dreams because they do not put forth the effort and have the self-discipline to do the little things it takes in order to achieve those dreams and goals.

Men who are undisciplined are slaves to their appetites, moods, and desires. Freedom comes from discipline. Self-discipline involves acting on how you *think* and not how you *feel*. If you allow your whims (your feelings—moods, appetites, desires) to control you, life is not of your own choosing.

Living a life with discipline is a much more efficient way to live life. It makes life easier and less chaotic. For instance, a lack of discipline in getting up for work or school causes a young man to oversleep. This causes him to be late, which causes him to rush, which means he neglects his appearance or forgets his lunch, which ultimately causes him to suffer in some way later in the day. Forgetting his lunch causes him to be hungry or to mooch off others or to spend money he didn't need to spend. Neglecting his appearance can lead to all sorts of problems—after all you only get one chance to make a first impression.

Here's just one reason our personal appearance matters: because people tend to judge us very quickly, especially on first impressions. This can be very important when trying to get accepted into a college or succeed at a job interview. I recently met a young man at an event where I spoke. He came up to me very excited, wanting to meet me and talk. He shared that he had recently given his heart to Christ and that my talk had been very inspiring to him. It was obvious he came from a very difficult background and had never had positive male role models to teach him even the simplest things in life. He wore tattered, grungy clothing and had an unkempt appearance. His lack of interpersonal communication skills and manners were readily apparent. He violated my personal space, continuously getting in my face. This would not have been so bad except he had very poor personal hygiene, especially his dental hygiene. His breath was terrible—and not because he'd been eating onions! Also, he tended to dominate the conversation to the point where I was uninterested in continuing to talk with him; he was much more interested in telling me what he knew instead of asking about what I knew.

This young man was not intentionally rude; he had just never been taught correct manners. It was not his fault! But unfortunately, he will pay the price for his ignorance. With no interpersonal communication skills, bad manners, and poor personal hygiene, it will be difficult for him to get a livable-wage job. In addition, men who could help him will be reluctant to spend time around him. These are all things he should have been taught while growing up, yet circumstances prevented him from benefiting from proper childhood training (or "home training" as my friends down South call it).

But having discipline allows us to anticipate problems and be prepared. I know if I am packed and ready to go a day before my flight, I am ready for any last-minute problems (of which there are always some). If I wait until the last minute to pack, I inevitably forget something. (You only need to forget your speaking notes once to understand the importance of being prepared.)

Being disciplined also allows us the opportunity to be ready when opportunities knock. Oftentimes when an opportunity presents itself we are not prepared to take advantage of it, especially if we have not been employing self-discipline in our lives. People who were debt free and had savings were in a great position to take advantage of fantastic prices on everything from homes to automobiles during the recent economic downturn. Those who were previously financially undisciplined could not take advantage of those opportunities.

At its worst, lack of discipline leads young men into trouble with the law and other failures in life that cause great regrets. Currently, about 15 percent (one out of every seven) of young men born since 1980 will spend time in prison. For young black men who do not attend college, about one out of every three will spend time in prison.[5] Often lack of self-discipline is one of the major factors that cause young males to make choices that land them in prison. More than ever we need men of self-control in our age of excess.

How to Teach Your Son Self-Discipline

> If unwilling to rise in the morning, say to thyself, "I awake to do the work of a man."
>
> —Marcus Aurelius

Too many young men in our culture are pre-adult boy-men who present themselves to the world as failures (we call them slackers) because they feel like failures as men or do not feel like men at all. They present a mask of being slovenly, uncaring of the world around them, unmotivated, and apathetic about anything except their own self-gratification. They appear to have a low sense of responsibility, low self-esteem, and little sense of honor. They have unconsciously decided to avoid becoming a man. Psychologist Michael Gurian describes these young men like this: "Like many 'pre-adult' males in our culture, most in their twenties or early thirties, he was a 'guy' raised without a father or enough male mentors, and/or in a position of poverty or wealthy entitlement that impeded his development into a mature man. He knew himself as a second or third rate male, not a man possessing what I would later discuss with him as a strong core-self."[6]

We need to teach our boys to be self-motivated. Part of being self-disciplined is being self-motivated. Many young men in our culture seem to have just given up. They'd rather play video games than go out and conquer the world—or even get a job. This epidemic of under-motivated boys and young men seems to be growing.

This "male lethargy" may be the result of a number of factors. Potential causes may include the following:

1. The large amount of estrogen receptors in plastics, pesticides, and other chemicals we are exposed to in greater concentrations today have lowered male sperm counts throughout the industrialized world. Researchers believe that the parts of male brains wired for testosterone receptors are not receiving the chemical balance they need, which ends up lowering male motivation.

2. Higher amounts of chemical toxins ingested by mothers during pregnancy are affecting the male fetus. Researchers are seeing higher incidents of genetic-based disorders such as autism and ADHD in young males than ever before.

3. A lack of father influence and male mentors is affecting the male motivation to succeed, learn, and mature. Boys without motivated mentors see no important male future and become lethargic in a world that does not seem to need boys or men very much.

4. Public schools may be contributing to under-motivation of males by not understanding male learning styles. Classes taught in verbal-emotive modalities are suited more for female than male learners. Males either fail or find much of what they learn is irrelevant, and rebel against school. This rebellion further erodes their ability to learn and motivation to succeed.

5. Parents are doing too much for their sons. When parents do not demand work and high character from their sons, it delays their maturation. (It's much easier being a boy than a man. Why grow up if you don't have to?).[7]

One of the keys to learning to be self-disciplined is to experience the consequences (especially the negative ones) of our choices—to not be rescued or bailed out whenever we have a problem. Another way we learn self-discipline is by *being* disciplined. Fathers are especially important in disciplining boys. Fathers seem to have been endowed by God with the mantle of authority within the family. Children have an innate fear factor of their fathers that they don't have with their mothers. The greater size, strength, and potential for violence men have compared to women contribute to this fright. Author Edmund Morris describes it thus: "There hung about his big, relaxed body an ever-present threat of violence, like that of a lion who, dozing, will suddenly flick out a lethal paw."[8]

For all boys, but especially for teen boys, fathers are the boundary that keeps them from asserting their will in ways that could be destructive to themselves and others. Fathers are routinely viewed as the enforcer of family rules and values. You seldom see gang members with involved, loving fathers at home. Teenage boys may even become disrespectful with Mom in ways they would never try with their father.

Boys who are not disciplined by their fathers do not learn self-discipline and self-control, which are huge factors in male satisfaction in life. Boys who are undisciplined are unhappy and grow up to be men who disappoint themselves and others in their lives.

Like most of the other traits mentioned in this book, the most important key to teaching your son self-discipline is to hold him accountable for his actions, choices, and decisions. So many people never learn that they hold their destiny in their own hands. The habits we establish, the people we associate with, the willingness we have to continue to learn, our attitude, and our willingness to be responsible for our decisions all contribute to our ability to succeed in life and in our relationships. The earlier we recognize that *we* are responsible for our happiness and lot in life instead of blaming others, the sooner and easier it is to get to work on the business of creating a satisfying life. We also need to recognize that one bad decision inevitably leads to another. And so one poor choice often leads to a whole series of bad choices in life—it becomes very hard to dig ourselves out of the hole we end up in.

Another factor in developing self-discipline is organization. It takes self-discipline to be organized. All men who accomplish great things seem to have the common traits of being organized and extremely well-disciplined.

Time organization and management are forms of self-discipline. Coach John Wooden had every minute of every practice mapped out in advance. Former Miami Dolphins coach Don Shula had every day on his calendar mapped out at least thirty days in advance.[9]

Self-discipline requires us to do things we do not want to do. It also requires us to *not* do things we'd like to do. I have to get out of bed and go to work most days. I work from home, so that requires even more self-discipline; I'd prefer to stay in bed all day or go live in a shack on a beach somewhere. But people depend on me to earn an income so they can eat and have a roof over their heads. The key is to teach our sons to discipline themselves in the things they need to do so that they can be allowed to do the things they want to do.

But having self-discipline in the small things in life may be of even greater importance. Not saying something that you *really* feel like saying to someone because it will hurt their feelings is a form of self-discipline. Paying my bills on time even if it means going without coffee for a week is self-discipline. Telling my boss off at work when I quit my job burns bridges that may (will) come back to haunt me later in life. Watching television every night instead of taking a college course prevents me from getting ahead at work. Teach your son the simple lesson of completing his work (homework, chores, and so on) *before* he plays. That's a life lesson that will serve him well throughout his life.

Perhaps the best way to teach boys self-discipline is to teach them the value of work—to ensure they have a good work ethic. *Work ethic* is the principle that hard work is intrinsically virtuous or worthy of reward. It is a belief in the moral value, benefit, and importance of work and its inherent ability to strengthen character.

It is healthy on many levels for males to work. God created the desire inside each man to want to provide for his wife and children. He feels great contentment and satisfaction when he is able to provide for them adequately. This is a natural instinct and not vanity. It is implanted in him by God for a divine purpose—to ensure that families will be adequately cared for.[10] Men who do not work (either intentionally or unintentionally) suffer because of it. They tend to have lower self-esteem and higher incidents of psychological problems, such as depression and anxiety. In addition, their wives and children have less respect for them. Women tend to have stronger emotional attachments to men when they feel provided for and protected. Lack of protection diminishes femininity.[11]

Your son needs to know and appreciate the value of work. No one who succeeds in life does so without working hard. However, the Protestant work ethic that made this country the greatest in the history of civilization may have run its course. There truly seems to be an entitlement mentality in this country.

So how do we change this reality and raise young men who are eager to make a difference in the world, who can be depended upon to provide for their wives and children? We can start by giving them chores from an early age. Give your son chores as part of his role in the family. You might give him a weekly allowance to teach him how to budget money, but he should do some chores with no compensation just because he's part of the family and they need to be done. They should be age appropriate, but don't be afraid to make them difficult and even physically challenging. You can always find other physical work that needs to be done around the home to pay him for if you want to keep his household chores and allowance separate. I had a wonderful decade or so when I didn't have to mow the lawn after I taught my son to cut the grass at age eleven.

Teach him to work—he's going to have to work for most of his life. The earlier you teach him the principles that help him be successful at work, the easier his life will be. I'd consider making your teenage son work outside the home. One of the major conflicts I hear from parents is whether to allow their children to experience positive extracurricular activities in school or to make them go to work. We experienced the same dilemma. We chose to allow our son to be in band, play sports, be in Boy Scouts, attend youth group at church, and be involved in student government at school because they were healthy, wholesome activities that kept him out of trouble. We purposely told him as long as he got good grades he did not have to work outside the home. And so we provided a car for transportation along with insurance—a major mistake we didn't make with our second child. Those extracurricular activities are important, but he probably didn't need to do all of them. In hindsight, he would have been better served to have worked for a boss and learned what working for minimum wage is like so that when he went into the world he would have appreciated the value of an education and been better prepared to take care of himself. Additionally, being forced to work to pay for his own car and insurance would have been an excellent way to teach him the value of those items. Our daughter did and was much the better for it.

We do our sons a great disservice when we do not teach them the value of hard work. I believe that part of a male's identity is created from the very act of work and (healthy or not) from the type of occupation he holds.

Many of the problems parents experience with their sons (of all ages) can be solved through work. Give your son chores, make him get a part-time job, and keep him physically active. He'll have fewer problems with his attitude, with getting into trouble, and with sex if you can keep him mentally and physically tired. The military discovered many years ago that they could eliminate fighting, horseplay, and sexual preoccupation in boot camp by keeping hundreds of teenagers and young men so physically exhausted that they fell asleep as soon as their heads hit the pillow in the barracks at night.

Boys develop the confidence and competency that define their self-esteem by accomplishing masculine chores that increase their skills and abilities. They learn this best under the guidance of a father or other older male. Masculine chores include activities like building things, doing yard work, pouring cement, repairing a car, fixing up a home, painting a house, repairing a roof, doing plumbing, or any number of other activities that are best accomplished by his own two hands, his muscular physique, and the sweat of his brow.

Finally, teach your son the self-discipline of delayed gratification, particularly economic self-discipline. The ability to wait and save money to purchase whatever he wants and needs with cash—especially in today's "gotta-have-it-now," instant gratification world—will bless him (and his family) his entire life. The recent economic recession caught many people unaware and has resulted in loss of homes, personal bankruptcy, and even the breakup of families. All because people were overextended on their credit—they were living beyond their means. Our culture has become so accustomed to using credit to purchase whatever we think we desire, that the idea of delayed gratification (or living within one's means) is almost laughable. Certainly it seems outdated and parochial. Yet think about how different your life might be if you were debt free. You'd have much less stress, you would have more flexibility in life, you'd be able to take advantage of opportunities when they occur (that special deal on a vacation to a tropical island)—in essence, you'd be free!

You can teach your son about delayed gratification by modeling it for him, of course. But another way is to pay him an allowance

Tips for Teaching Boys Self-Discipline

- Teach him to be grateful—not feel entitled. Teaching him to say "Please" and "Thank you" often encourages gratefulness. Giving thanks in prayer also develops a grateful attitude.
- Teach him to fast. This is also an activity that requires and teaches self-discipline (although it's one I admit to being weak in). Fasting is not only practiced in a religious context but is used by various men who want to develop their discipline and willpower. In addition, you can fast from anything—it doesn't have to be food. It could be TV, video games, shopping, or anything else you want to learn discipline with.
- Teach him to control his emotions. Teach him the value of cultivating positive emotions like love, hope, and faith in his life instead of being mastered by negative emotions such as jealousy, hatred, and greed.
- Teach him to manage his time effectively. This self-discipline will benefit him greatly throughout his life.

for chores and then require him to use his own money to buy the things he wants (not necessities—as a parent you still need to provide food, shelter, and clothing). Don't loan him any money or advance his allowance. Help him identify expenses or events that are coming up for which he might need to save his income. If you go to church, teach him the importance of tithing. Teach him the value of consistently saving a portion of his allowance. Also, teach him to wait before making a decision to buy something. When I want to buy something I generally wait a day or two before making a purchase. It's surprising how often I decide I don't really need or even want what I *had* to have.

Dads, it will be important for you to be a bit "hard" on your son. Moms are frequently tougher on daughters than they are on sons. Most mothers allow their sons to get away with things they would never allow their daughters to get away with. It is imperative that you teach him the value of self-discipline even if it means being what might appear to be "mean" to him in some circumstances. If your experience is anything like mine, your wife won't be happy about that sometimes, but it is in your son's best interest. Men and boys without self-discipline seldom reach their potential. And oftentimes the only way boys learn self-discipline is by having it forced upon them.

6

Perseverance

Abraham Lincoln

*Champions are not those who never fail, but those who
never quit.*

—Edwin Louis Cole, *Never Quit*

*Our greatest glory is not in never failing, but in rising
up every time we fail.*

—Ralph Waldo Emerson

PERSEVERANCE IS STEADY PERSISTENCE, OR A DOGGED
tenacity to overcome obstacles. It is the continued effort to
do or achieve something despite difficulties, failure, or opposition. It is the tendency to continue forward in pursuit of a goal
without external motivation or reward. Perseverance is determination, dedication, and endurance in the face of trials and adversity.
It is not quitting even when things seem impossible.

Perhaps no man achieved more after starting out with less through
sheer perseverance than did Abraham Lincoln.

Abraham Lincoln—Man of Perseverance

Abraham Lincoln (1809–1865) was the sixteenth president of the United States. He led the country through the greatest constitutional, military, and moral crisis our country has ever faced—the American Civil War.

Lincoln's mother died when he was nine years old. Lincoln was almost entirely self-educated; he received only eighteen months of formal schooling. He offset this disadvantage by voraciously consuming any book he could get his hands on. During his youth, Lincoln became an adept axman in his work building rail fences and gained a reputation for brawn and audacity during competitive wrestling matches (although unlike the book and movie there is no evidence he was a vampire hunter).

At age twenty-two, he packed his meager belongings in a canoe and paddled out on his own. He taught himself law and became a successful attorney and state legislator in Illinois. As a frontier lawyer he rode the circuit from town to town, providing whatever legal services were needed. During his years as an attorney he met many political and business leaders, earning a reputation as an honest and capable lawyer (hence the nickname "Honest Abe").

He was tall (6'4") with long arms and legs, and was considered ugly by many critics who described him as a "scarecrow" or a "gorilla." He also reportedly had a high-pitched voice, yet was an uncanny orator, who used warmth, his sense of humor, and modesty to win over audiences. He was a poor student yet loved to read and would often walk for miles to borrow books from neighbors. Later in life, Lincoln became deeply religious but never formally joined a church.[1]

Lincoln knew success and failure. He failed in several business ventures. He was a one-term member of the United States House of Representatives but was defeated for other legislative, congressional, and senate seats several times.

Lincoln lacked everything we think we need to be successful in life—connections, powerful friends, charisma, good looks, and formal education—and yet became one of the greatest presidents in United States history. Born in a one-room cabin to uneducated farmer parents, Abraham Lincoln's rise to the presidency has long been the stuff of legend. Losing to Stephen Douglas in the 1858 senatorial election did not deter Lincoln from his goals; he persevered against this same opponent to win the presidential election in 1860.

Lincoln encountered difficulties from the very beginning of his presidency. As soon as he was elected, seven states seceded from the Union. During the war, Lincoln focused on both the military and political dimensions of the conflict. While closely supervising the war effort, Lincoln always kept in mind the goal of reunifying the nation. His policies were opposed from almost every direction, yet Lincoln persevered.

The rest, of course, is history. Lincoln went on to guide America through her darkest and stormiest hours, facing challenges no other president has encountered. Lincoln has been consistently ranked by scholars and the public as one of the three greatest US presidents. Six days after the Confederacy surrendered, Lincoln was shot and killed by John Wilkes Booth.

Lincoln admitted he failed a lot, but he never quit. He never considered himself a quitter or a failure. He learned from his losses and mistakes. His persistence in the face of great adversity contributed to his toughness, built his character, and hardened his will. He learned perseverance, humility, strength, determination, and wisdom from his failings. His failures prepared him to be uniquely qualified to lead an entire country gripped in the most desperate of circumstances at a time when it was being torn apart from within. That's the kind of men we need to produce today as our country faces challenges that threaten to tear us apart again.

Why Perseverance Is Important

> Never, never, never, never give up.
>
> —Winston Churchill

Life is difficult. And the things that mean the most in life are the hardest. In fact, anything worth doing is difficult. There's just no way around it. Failure is never final—unless you quit. Unfortunately, quitting is an easily learned habit by young males. We learn early in life to take the easiest route and avoid anything unpleasant. Boys who are rescued too often learn to quit. Then anytime something becomes difficult in life they quit or take pains to avoid it. They become conditioned or programmed to expect someone else (generally a woman) to come along and take care of it for them. Boys like this struggle throughout life and the people who depend on them suffer most.

What does this look like in real life? Let me ask some questions to illustrate this point. How difficult is marriage? It's very difficult in my experience. How hard is raising a family? Raising a family may be one of the toughest tasks on the planet. How about working at a job you hate in order to feed your family? From experience I know it is extremely difficult. So for a boy who's learned to quit, what happens the first time marriage becomes difficult? He quits. What about when raising his family is hard? He leaves. How about having to work a job he hates to feed his family? Often, a man without the quality of perseverance quits, causing his family to suffer economic, if not psychological, hardships.

Your son needs to learn that people will depend upon him his entire life. His wife and children will need him to be dependable and dedicated to their well-being. His coworkers or employees will depend upon him for their livelihood. And if you've read any of my other books for men you know that I believe men have been endowed with the God-given ability to enrich and lift up others to become more than they could possibly be. But this ability requires a certain commitment and dedication.

My friend, Pat Williams, author and senior vice president of the Orlando Magic, talks about the "Dirty Shoulders" principle. All great people have dirty shoulders from lifting others up and letting them stand tall on their shoulders.[2] They don't mind if they don't get credit; they just want to lift others up. Most of the great leaders highlighted in this book were well known for encouraging, guiding, and molding the people around them to achieve great things. Their steadfastness and dedication were like a foundation others could stand upon to look out over the horizon above the challenges of life.

To have perseverance is to have a certain measure of steadfastness and dedication. The roots of the word *steadfast* are "stead" (place) and "fast" (fixed, unmoving). To be steadfast requires a man to be fixed in place like a wall of dependability. Our country needs men who will stand fast against evil. Our culture has been slowly and steadily grinding away the moral values that make civilization work. Men who stand firm for traditional values and moral integrity face challenges today. We are attacked when we stand for what is virtuous, good, and moral. Boys especially are made fun of if they are considered too "wholesome." Perhaps it's because those of us who live life using godly philosophies (just by our presence alone) stand as a form of accusation against people who live lives apart from Christ. It seems that anytime a person tries to live a superior life, others line up to try to tear him down. In the alcoholic home I was raised in, I was accused of thinking I was "better" than my parents because I chose to live a different lifestyle than they lived. My parents seemed to relish my failures and be resentful of my successes.

In our culture today, we see many examples of those who love evil condemning those who stand for righteousness and godly principles. (Just watch the nightly news.) They then protect the perpetrators of sin and wickedness. They laud them as being "open-minded," "enlightened," or even as a "victim of their circumstances." All the while accusations fly against those who are holy and just. Good is bad and bad is good. The Evil One attempts to "make dirty those who are pure, to make cowards of those who show courage, to cause to bend or bow those who stand up for God."[3] Pat Williams describes it this way: "In our age, ego and arrogance are celebrated, and humility is often confused with self-abasement."[4]

That continuous cultural onslaught requires a man to be resolutely faithful or he will eventually cave in. He will become depleted physically, emotionally drained, mentally depressed, and ready to give up unless he is adamant and unwavering in his commitments. He will fall prey to life's temptations of infidelity, apathy, and pride. His allegiance to what is right must be enduring and staunch. He must be relentless in his pursuit of honorable stability or he will fall like a once-mighty oak tree and those who depend on him will be washed away like the eroded banks of a stream. Without the traits of steadfastness and dedication, he and those who depend upon him will fall.

It's part of God's plan that we learn to persevere through difficult times. It builds our character and our faith. Author Randy Alcorn says, "God could create scientists, mathematicians, athletes, and musicians. He doesn't. He creates children who take on those roles over a long process. We learn to excel by handling failure. Only in cultivating discipline, endurance, and patience do we find satisfaction and reward."[5]

Boys who have learned to quit never become effective leaders, they never become heroes. They never accomplish anything worthwhile because they do not have the intestinal fortitude to continue on when things are tough. They have learned to quit and avoid anything unpleasant like it was the plague. Being professional (no matter what we do) means playing the hand you are dealt. Life is difficult. Quitting never solved anything.

Ralph Waldo Emerson said, "The characteristic of heroism is its persistency. All men have wandering impulses, fits, and starts of generosity. But when you have chosen your part, abide by it, and do not weakly try to reconcile yourself with the world. The heroic cannot be the common, nor the common the heroic."[6]

Additionally, boys who are rescued too often are never allowed to fail and thus never learn to persevere through difficulties until they achieve success. This process is what develops healthy self-esteem in males. By failing and then getting back up and persevering to success is how males feel adequate and competent—two very important factors in the healthy ego development of boys and men.

Perseverance is a battle a man has with himself. Author and early icon of the Christian men's movement, Ed Cole, said, "Whenever we are faced with difficult circumstances (trials, temptations, testing) the greatest challenges do not come from external foes or formidable circumstances, but from within our own soul."[7] Men who do not have the ability to persevere through difficult circumstances are unable to achieve anything of significance in life.

How to Teach Your Son Perseverance

Never think that God's delays are God's denials. Hold on; hold fast; hold out. Patience is genius.

—Georges-Louis Leclerc

A new study published in the *Journal of Early Adolescence* found that dads are in a unique position to instill persistence (perseverance) in their children, particularly in the preteen and teen years. Dads who model hard work and keep chipping away at pursuits they care about pass persistence along to their children. Researchers from Brigham Young University found that fathers who practiced authoritative parenting, defined as providing feelings of love, granting autonomy, and emphasizing accountability to a child, were more likely to have kids who developed the art of persistence, which led to better outcomes in school and lower instances of misbehavior. Researchers said the study joins a growing body of research that suggests fathers are uniquely important to children's self-regulation and self-esteem.[8]

Perseverance is probably one of the toughest traits to teach boys. It requires us resisting the urge to rescue them when they are struggling. It goes against our nature to let our children suffer, but suffer they must if they are to develop the strength for the long haul.

When my son, Frank, was in sixth grade, he decided he wanted to go out for the wrestling team. I had wrestled all through high school, so I knew what he would be getting himself into. Wrestling is a brutal sport, both physically and mentally. My son was a great kid, but he didn't have a mean bone in his body.

After we discussed some of the harder aspects of wrestling, such as doing hundreds of push-ups and sit-ups every day, running up and down stairs, practicing constantly, starving yourself to lose weight, and getting slammed to the mat repeatedly, he decided that he still wanted to try out. I had a firm rule with my kids—I didn't care what they attempted, but they had to stick with it for a reasonable amount of time, usually a season. I told him, "Okay, but you're not going to quit." So with that reminder in mind, Frank trundled on off to the wrestling team.

Frank was a big boy for his age, and since wrestlers are divided by weight classes, he naturally ended up wrestling eighth graders most of the time in practice. There can be a huge difference in muscle mass between sixth- and eighth-grade boys. Many eighth graders have been through puberty and are developing man-like muscles, even beards—most sixth graders haven't. Two weeks into the season, Frank wanted to quit. He was getting hurt by the older boys in practice. He was coming home every day bruised, battered, and even bleeding. One day he came to me and said, "Dad, the older boys are hurting me. I just don't want to be hurt anymore!

Please, can I quit?" It broke my heart to have to look into Frank's teary eyes and tell him he couldn't quit. He was going to have to suck it up and be a man, to finish what he started. I prayed many times to God to confirm that I was doing the right thing.

To make matters worse, my wife was giving me the "look." You know that look. The one that says you're going to be sleeping outside with the dog if this goes badly.

To make a long story short, I made Frank stay on the team. Several weeks later, in his first wrestling match, he was paired against a young fellow about his age and maturity level. During the first two rounds and most of the third, Frank was tossed around the mat like a chew toy in the jaws of a puppy. His main strategy was to adopt a turtle-like posture on his belly—probably a learned defense mechanism from wrestling older and bigger boys in practice. Survival was his only goal. However, toward the end of the match, his opponent, apparently exhausted from pushing Frank's weight around the mat, inexplicably dropped and rolled over onto his back. Frank looked up in surprise, fell on top of him, and pinned him with seconds to go! Suddenly, Frank's whole countenance changed. He jumped up, dancing around the ring like Muhammad Ali, on his toes with his arms in the air.

But as we made eye contact across the gym, I knew he had learned the joy of persevering through difficulties and hard work and discovered the rewards that come from not quitting. The hours of hard work and pain had paid off. The reward was his because he had not quit when the going was tough. And the reward was that much sweeter—like cool, clear water, refreshing his parched soul—because of the agonies he'd endured.

Had I made the decision whether or not to allow him to quit the wrestling team based on my feelings instead of my principles he might have failed to learn an important life lesson. I did not *feel* like making him stay on the team, but the principle said it was the right thing to do. The principle required *me* to have the courage to make the right decision and stand by it (even though others in my family may not have thought it was the right thing to do) and then be willing to suffer the consequences of my decision. It also required me to fight through the alluring pull of my feelings and make a decision using a sound principle, instead of making the easy choice in order to assuage my own troubling emotions over the situation. It was a fantastic life lesson for Frank on the value of perseverance.

James 1:12 says, "Blessed is the man who perseveres under trial, because when he has stood the test, he will receive the crown of life that God has promised to those who love him" (NIV 1984). Not allowing our sons to quit too easily is one way we teach them the trait of perseverance. Allowing them to suffer the natural consequences of their decisions is another.

As we look back on how we raised our children, one of the biggest regrets my wife and I have is that we probably rescued our kids too much—we did not allow them to suffer the consequences of their actions. Because of the hardships we both endured in childhood, we wanted to prevent our children from experiencing those disadvantages and so we often rescued them from situations where we should have let them suffer the consequences of their actions. It's a lesson I talk a lot about with moms, who have a natural inclination to want to rescue their sons. Here's one example: While I think it is important to be an advocate for your child, we might have advocated *too* much for ours. We did not let them suffer the natural consequences of situations like not doing their homework, failing to follow through on projects, not practicing for sports hard enough, or even not doing their chores on time (we would capitulate and allow them to attend an important event even if they did not do what they were supposed to do). They never had to miss a meal because they forgot to take their lunch or walk to school because they missed the bus. They literally did not learn to fear consequences because we never allowed them to fail.

Letter from a Single Mom

Hi Rick,

I just wanted to share that I am keeping in the front of my mind what you have said about moms not rescuing their sons. And, all the while, I've been slightly amazed at the number of people encouraging me to do just that.

My son learned early in middle school that not turning assignments in on time was okay. Most of his teachers allowed him to turn in late assignments with no reduction in grade up until the last day of the trimester. He has continued to do that in 8th grade despite reminders and encouragement from his teachers (and me) to turn in assignments on time. His belief was "it is only middle school, it doesn't matter."

Oh, but it does matter as he found out this past week. He applied to an exclusive private high school. He was one of 350 who applied and one of the 150 accepted . . . but his acceptance was contingent upon not having any grade below a C- for the rest of the year. He soon discovered that middle school grades do matter! He missed turning in two assignments in a class and ended up with a D (his first D) . . . which means he loses the opportunity to go to the private school.

Many people have told me to talk with the teacher and see if she will allow him to do something so that the grade can be changed to a C. And, as much as I believe this school would have been a good opportunity for him, I keep telling myself that he needs to accept responsibility for his actions and live with the consequences. Learning can be tough. I am sad that he will not be able to attend the private school and praying that God will somehow turn this into a good experience.

Thank you for giving support to do the right thing even when it would be easier in the short term for me to try to fix this.

I recently heard a politician say on a television interview, "There are only two ways to fail in our country—quit or die." He knows that perseverance is what separates people who succeed from those who fail. We only truly learn to persevere by being held accountable for the choices and decisions we make. There's no easy way to develop this trait.

However, having a positive attitude makes persevering through tough times more enjoyable. Teach your son to look on the bright side of things—to look for the silver lining. Teach him to give people the benefit of the doubt. Most people are so wrapped up in their own issues that when they hurt or slight others, it is not intentional. Teach him to have a good sense of humor and to have compassion for others. Teach him the importance of being faithful, punctual, thorough, diligent, honest, and generous. If he is all those things he will be happy and others will enjoy being around him. That will make the tough times in life easier to persevere through.

Last, because perseverance requires the ability to accept responsibility for our actions, choices, and decisions, help your son understand that as long as a person is blaming someone else for his problems, he is not a leader—he is a victim. Victims are the opposite of leaders. Victims are passive; they are acted *upon*. Leaders take the initiative to make something happen.

Part of the problem in our culture is that so many want to blame someone else for their problems—they seldom take personal responsibility for how their lives turn out. This is prevalent even in the small areas of life. My wife and I were just in a restaurant. Her steak was very undercooked so she sent it back to the kitchen. The manager came over and was very nice (comping my wife's meal) but literally could not force herself to blame the staff for the mistake. She finally concluded that the waitress misunderstood my wife when she said she wanted her meat cooked "medium well," the implication being it was somehow my wife's fault instead of the restaurant's.

Interestingly, it's common knowledge that people who are happy and successful in life are those who have an internal thought process that takes responsibility for their lives and actions. People who are not successful tend to commiserate on their problems and look for others to blame.

Your son deserves to at least have a chance at a happy, successful, productive, fulfilled life. His best chance to achieve that is by learning to be accountable for his own decisions and persevere through life's challenges.

7

Hardihood and Resiliency

Jedediah Smith

I hate to have to tell you this, but whether you like it or not, you're a man, you're stuck with it. You'll find yourself standing your ground and fighting when you ought to run, speaking out when you ought to keep your mouth shut, doing things that will seem wrong to a lot of people, but you'll do 'em all the same.

—JOHN WAYNE, *The Train Robbers*

The fading of the warrior contributes to the collapse of civilized society. A man who cannot defend his own space cannot defend women and children.

—ROBERT BLY, *Iron John*

HARDIHOOD IS AN INTERNAL TOUGHNESS THAT IS COM-prised of equal parts resiliency, resolute courage, fortitude, and self-assured audacity. It empowers vigor, robustness, and physical endurance by allowing a person to ignore the first onset of fatigue. It causes a person to willingly meet the challenges of life without having to be emotionally inspired or stimulated. It means being both mentally and physically rugged.

Hardihood requires mental toughness. It gives a man the courage to withstand rebuffs while remaining indifferent to criticism and opposition. The mental and emotional effect of this characteristic is an immense advantage in life. Sensitivity to the opinions of others has caused many men who might otherwise be most capable to fail. A man who cares too much about what others think of him or his actions is prone to suffer from a lack of hardihood.[1]

Being resilient is the ability to be able to recover from something quickly—either physically (such as an impact) or psychologically (like adversity or misfortune). It is the ability to bounce back from illness, depression, discouragement, disappointment, or stress. In children, resiliency helps them resist peer pressure and high risk factors, especially after being exposed to a high level of trauma.

Jedediah Smith embodied the character traits of hardihood and resiliency.

Jedediah Smith—Portrait of Hardihood

Jedediah Strong Smith (1799–1831) was a nineteenth-century hunter, trapper, fur trader, trailblazer, author, cartographer, and explorer of the Rocky Mountains, the American Southwest and West Coast. Smith was the first white man to travel overland from the Salt Lake frontier, across the Colorado River, the Mojave Desert, and into California. He was also the first to explore and cross the Sierra Nevada and the Great Basin. Smith was the first American to travel up the California coast to reach the Oregon Country. He and Robert Stuart discovered the South Pass, which became the main route used by pioneers to travel to the Oregon Country. In his short lifetime, Smith traveled more extensively in unknown territory than any other mountain man.

Legendary trappers and explorers such as Zebulon Pike, Kit Carson, and Jim Bridger along with famous frontiersmen like Davy Crockett and Daniel Boone all exhibited the character trait of hardihood. We admire these men because they faced life in an untamed world with little more than their wits and bare hands. They made what they needed and fixed what broke. They faced death many times.

Smith stood out even among his peers. His explorations helped open expansion of the American West.

In 1824, while looking for the Crow tribe to obtain fresh horses and westward directions, Jedediah Smith was stalked and attacked by a large grizzly bear. The huge bear jumped and tackled him to the ground. Smith's ribs were broken and members of his party witnessed Smith fighting the bear, which ripped open his side with its claws and took his head in its mouth. The bear suddenly retreated and the men ran to help Smith. They found his scalp and ear nearly ripped off, but he convinced a friend to sew it loosely back on, giving him directions on how to do it. After resting for two weeks to recuperate from his bloody wounds and broken ribs, Smith resumed leadership of the expedition. He wore his hair long the rest of his life to cover the large scar from his eyebrow to his ear.[2]

On his first expedition in 1826, Smith attempted to find new beaver hunting grounds along the Colorado River. After a difficult pass through the mountains into the Mojave Desert, the party was attacked by a group of Mohave Indians and lost several men. Eventually they traveled into California to get supplies for the return trip home and were arrested by the Mexican army. After agreeing to leave California, they were released but stayed instead and explored the San Joaquin Valley.

By early 1827 Smith and his party had accumulated over fifteen hundred pounds of beaver, but getting the fur to the "mountain man rendezvous" near Great Salt Lake was a problem. Smith traveled 350 miles north but could not find a break in the wall of the

Sierra. Turning up a rugged canyon of what would later be called the American River (named after his party), he began to cross the mountains. The heavy snow was too deep and forced him to return to the Stanislaus River in order to save his men and horses. Smith then took two men and some extra horses and began what would become his epic crossing of the Sierra Nevada farther south. He hoped for a quick rendezvous so he could return to his party with more men later in the year. After crossing the Sierra Nevada, Smith continued east across central Nevada straight through some of the most difficult desert in North America—the Great Basin. One man, Robert Evans, collapsed and could not continue. Smith briefly left Evans and pressed on until he found some water and returned to rescue Evans. The three eventually all reached Great Salt Lake.

The following year, Smith returned to California with eighteen men and two women. At the Colorado River, the party was attacked again by the Mojave, killing ten men and taking the two women. The party moved north to meet with the group that had been left in the San Joaquin Valley the year before. Smith was once again arrested by the Mexican government near Monterrey, California. And again the governor released Smith on the promise that he leave the province immediately and not return. But as before, Smith and his party remained in California hunting in Sacramento Valley for several months before heading north along the Pacific Coast to use the Columbia River to return to their headquarters. Smith became the first explorer to reach the Oregon Country overland by traveling up the California coast.

In the Oregon Country, Smith's party got into a dispute with the Umpqua people over a stolen ax. Later, Smith's group was attacked and fifteen of Smith's nineteen men were killed. Smith managed to reach safety at the Hudson's Bay Company post at Fort Vancouver.[3] Smith decided to never enter Oregon Territory again.

Smith later led a trapping expedition into Blackfeet territory and successfully gathered a large amount of furs before being repulsed by a tribe of Blackfeet. He returned to St. Louis a wealthy man.

In 1831, Smith was leading supply wagons for the Rocky Mountain Fur Company on the Santa Fe Trail. According to Dale L. Morgan, Jedediah Smith's biographer, Smith was looking for water when he came upon an estimated fifteen to twenty Comanches. The Comanches scared his horse and shot him in the left shoulder. Smith wheeled his horse around and with a rifle shot was able to kill their chief. The Comanches rushed Smith and stabbed him to death with lances. Austin Smith, Jedediah's brother, was able to later retrieve Smith's rifle and pistols that the Indians had taken and traded to the Mexicans. Smith had died at the age of thirty-two.

Though he was an accomplished outdoorsman, Smith did not fit the stereotype of the mountain man. He never drank, never used tobacco, never boasted, and was rarely humorous. Another rare quality was his faith. A Methodist, Smith was a reserved, pious man who often read the Bible, meditated, and prayed. Smith reportedly did not practice sexual relations with Native American women as many of his contemporaries did. Smith was known for his many accurately recorded observations on the nature and topography of areas he explored.

Smith accomplished much more than most men despite only living to be thirty-two years old. He accomplished those things because of his hardihood and resiliency in the face of adversity.

Why Hardihood and Resiliency Are Important

I don't know who you are. I don't know what you want. If you are looking for ransom, I can tell you I don't have money. But what I do have are a very particular set of skills—skills I have acquired over a very long career. Skills that make me a nightmare for people like you. If you let my daughter go now, that'll be the end of it. I will not look for you, I will not pursue you. But if you don't, I will look for you, I will find you, and I will kill you.

—Liam Neeson, *Taken*

105

In his book *Man of Steel and Velvet*, Aubrey Andelin describes the inner qualities of an authentic man as needing to be like both "steel and velvet"—the same term Carl Sandburg used to describe Abraham Lincoln. As Andelin says, these are the qualities that "shape a man's destiny, impel him to success as a husband, father and builder of society."[4] He posits that men need a balance of both the tough, hard strength, endurance, and tempering of fine steel as well as the soft gentleness, tenderness, generosity, and patience of velvet in order to be effective leaders. Too much steel and men may make their mark in history but risk becoming dictators like Caesar, Stalin, Hitler, and Mussolini. Too much velvet and men never achieve greatness. As he says, "There are scores of men throughout history who have been *velvet* men. Although they do not stand out as enemies to society, they do not stand out for anything else. They are nonentities, being remembered for nothing of note. Not being real men, they did not build a better world, nor were they adequate as family leaders."[5]

A long-running TV commercial by an automobile insurance company asked the question, "Does a former drill sergeant make a terrible therapist?" The commercial shows a sensitive, sniveling young man lying on a couch telling a former DI that the color yellow makes him sad. The DI proceeds to thoroughly chew him out before finally calling him a crybaby and throwing a box of tissues at him in disgust. That commercial is funny, but I was talking to a friend of mine who has served on active duty in the military for the past fifteen years. He mentioned that many young men now coming into the military are sensitive, soft, and have a tendency to cry easily, exactly like the young man portrayed in that commercial. He noted that it was sad because these young men were being brutalized by the rigors, traditions, and rough-hewn requirements of the military. His comment was that the new "softer" or feminized version of masculinity is not suited for the mental, emotional, and physical toughness required to be a warrior.

All boys and men (even sensitive ones) need some degree of mettle and intestinal fortitude to succeed in life. They need these traits because life is hard. Someday their families will depend on them. Some may even have employees, troops, or whole communities that rely on them to be strong and have endurance for the long haul. Our culture needs men who are willing to meet difficult challenges head-on and avoid the path of least resistance.

In order to fulfill his role and responsibilities in life a man needs hardihood. Not only that, but he must also have the ability to physically protect his family if necessary. Life can be brutal and a man needs to shoulder great burdens throughout its trials. Life often requires us to be aggressive, decisive, and independent in order to succeed. Overcoming life's challenges requires men to be competent, fearless, steadfast, and dedicated. Softness and timidity are the enemies of successful leadership. With the character trait of hardihood comes confidence and peace because a man knows he can withstand and endure anything life throws at him.

Resiliency develops over time as we face difficulties and persevere through them. It allows us to make a positive adaptation or outcome from a negative situation or circumstance and to cope well under adversity. Much like hardihood, it enables us to continue on despite whatever hardships we face.

But sometimes resiliency is simply a choice we make. My wife left home at age thirteen. She came from a single parent home that was awash with alcoholism, emotional and sexual abuse, and poverty. She escaped from that environment only to suffer many other dangerous and difficult challenges in a world that frequently chews up and spits out thirteen-year-old girls after wringing every drop of humanity and dignity from them. Yet she turned out remarkably unscathed—she was resilient. Much like a rubber ball that bounces back and retains its original shape after being slammed against a concrete wall, she somehow retained her positive attitude despite the circumstances in which she was raised. She credits it to the fact that she made a decision not to follow in the footsteps that were modeled for her. Statistically, not many people are able to overcome generational cycles and childhood role modeling. But she dug deep within herself and gritted her way through the atrocities of life until she was capable of controlling her own destiny. Not only do I admire her pluck but I respect the dickens out of her as well. Where she obtained this resilient character she does not know, but it has served our marriage well in that she has been capable of withstanding the trials and tribulations that all long-term relationships face.

How to Teach Your Son Hardihood

Character cannot be developed in ease and quiet. Only through experience of trial and suffering can the soul be strengthened, ambition inspired, and success achieved.

—Helen Keller

As mentioned earlier in this book, we live in an instant gratification world. We expect our food to be prepared and delivered within minutes (or seconds) of its being ordered. We don't like discomfort and expect our needs to be fulfilled instantly. We expect pretty much any whim we have to be satisfied within moments or we become downright belligerent about it. That type of attitude does not do well with promoting and developing hardihood or resiliency.

So how do we develop the trait of hardihood? We develop it through suffering. It seems counterintuitive for most parents to make a choice to allow their children to suffer. But no other traits allow us to be successful more than hardihood and resiliency. Life is full of struggles, disappointments, and hurts. The ability to successfully overcome life's challenges in a productive way probably means the difference between a life worth living and one that is mere existence.

So how do we allow our children to suffer without traumatizing them? One way, as also mentioned earlier, is not to rescue them too often—to allow them to fail, persevere, and learn from their mistakes. Part of suffering is learning to accept responsibility for our own choices and decisions.

Since the beginning of time, moms have been using some variation of the line, "You'll poke your eye out!" to prevent boys from playing with anything they consider dangerous, whether it be a stick, a pencil, or a BB gun. I don't know for sure, but I would guess that perhaps maybe one boy in the entire history of the world has ever poked his eye out.

Let your boy take risks and even get hurt from time to time. Males learn best through trial and error, failing and persevering until they succeed. That's also how they develop healthy self-esteem. If boys are never allowed to fail (or worse are always recued) how are they ever supposed to learn life's most important lessons? How are they supposed to develop self-confidence and self-esteem? Boys don't acquire those traits by being *told* how wonderful they are— they acquire them by trying, failing, and ultimately succeeding at life's challenges. Let them get hurt. Boys thrive on roughhousing and being physical. Don't discourage that. Let him have a pocket knife—just teach him how to use it and the rules of knife ownership. He'll probably cut his fingers a few times, but that's what stitches are for. Besides, a scar is a boy's badge of honor. Also he should have a slingshot and a BB gun at the appropriate ages. Just teach him that the neighbor's cats are off limits.

Encourage your son to set high goals and attempt difficult endeavors. Encourage him to keep going even (especially) when he wants to quit. Don't let him settle for being average or even "normal." Most people never come close to reaching their full potential. For males especially the fear of failure keeps them from even trying. Teach your son to embrace failure, not to fear it. Encourage him to try difficult tasks even if he thinks he will fail. As

Words to Raise Boys By

Robert Scott was a heroic explorer in the early 1900s who made several trips to the Antarctic in an attempt to be the first one to reach the South Pole. He made it on his last attempt only to discover he had been beaten by just days by Roald Amundsen. Scott and his men never made it home, getting caught in a blizzard just miles from camp. As he lay dying he wrote a final letter to his wife where he makes known his wishes for their son, "I had looked forward to helping you to bring him up, but it is a satisfaction to know that he will be safe with you . . . Make the boy interested in natural history if you can. It is better than games. . . . I know you will keep him in the open air. Try to make him believe in God, it is comforting . . . and guard him against indolence. Make him a strenuous man. I had to force myself into being strenuous, as you know—had always an inclination to be idle."[6]

noted psychologist Michael Gurian says, "Boys and men learn and grow through confrontations and experiences that pit their sometimes meager resources against forces, beings, themes greater than themselves."[7]

Set up challenges (physical, mental, and emotional) for your son. Encourage him then to persevere through difficulties and find activities that stretch him—don't let him quit too easily. The pursuit of easy quests makes men weak. Most males tend to drift toward whatever job or pursuit is easiest for them. They avoid anything difficult. Too many males today are apathetic and complacent. They never attempt things that they don't think they can accomplish or that require great amounts of energy. Most males have a great fear of failing or looking incompetent. This keeps them from attempting great things in life.

Set goals to help motivate him. Motivation is a big part of getting young males to move beyond complacency. Topics that interest and motivate young males are themes such as masculinity, respect, and character. Young males are always searching for how a man acts, what character traits a man has, and how to be respected by other males. The young men we work with are very interested in what makes a man—they want to know how a man thinks, solves problems, and faces life. Most boys (and men) want to talk about bravery, battle, honor, manhood, character, and protection of others. Gurian says, "No matter how tough a male seems, he is constantly fragile because he is constantly measuring himself against the larger themes of manhood."[8]

Force your son to test himself—physically and mentally. Often boys must be forced to do things they do not want, as their initial inclination is to avoid anything unpleasant or difficult. He won't always like this but it will make him a better, stronger man. Help him set goals for himself and then a plan to achieve those goals. This is an ongoing activity. He should have daily goals (written down) as well as short-term and long-term goals. These goals might change year to year.

When our kids were growing up we always had a year-end list of goals that we would read to each other during our annual New Year's Eve dinner. We would review the goals we had set from the last year and discuss what we had accomplished, what we had not, and why. In addition to that we all had long-term goals such as what we wanted to be when we grew up, what we wanted to achieve in life, and what we wanted to accomplish but were afraid of trying.

Find activities that allow your son to experience "controlled aggression." The Boy Scouts allows boys to aggressively test themselves against each other, against nature, and against tasks designed to give them skills that will help build their self-confidence and self-esteem. Sports, science fairs, and music also provide competitive environments. For boys who are more cerebral, chess is a highly aggressive mental exercise. Most males thrive on competition.

Encourage him to undertake challenges at which he might fail. There is nothing that builds self-esteem and confidence in a boy or man like testing himself against great odds and coming out on top. That may require you as parents to push yourselves out of your comfort zone and do things that are difficult for you in order to support him in these activities. I can remember going snow caving with my son one winter on a Boy Scout campout. It was freezing cold and snowing. He had to burrow out a snow cave and use a candle as a heat source for our overnight sleeping accommodations. It was not something I was excited about doing, but after we completed it we felt good about it and it actually was pretty warm. Not only do both of us know we can survive the night in arctic conditions, but Frank now has the confidence to tackle other life challenges like being a husband and father because of his experiences. (If you can survive in the frozen wilderness, how tough can taking care of a family be?)

Exceptionalism and rugged-individualism helped make America the greatest country that has ever existed. Those traits are frowned upon or at least considered politically incorrect today. Multiculturalism tells us that no one culture is better than another. Yet one only has to look at the many civilizations (a word loosely used) around the world that have been in the "stone ages" for centuries— ones who murder their citizens, debase and brutalize women and children, and subjugate their members. There's nothing wrong with being proud of your country, heritage, job, or your family. And there's nothing wrong with wanting to raise our boys to be tough. Somehow our culture has determined that it is admirable for our boys to be sensitive and ignoble for them to be tough. That would appear to me to be a somewhat feminized perspective on masculinity. Boys need to be tough to successfully navigate through life's challenges. They need to be strong and reliable because someday people will depend on them. A boy may depend on others but a man stands on his own two feet and makes his own way. Frankly, if bad stuff is going down, I want men—police, soldiers, and so on—who will be tough, not sensitive, when dealing with it.

In 1836, American educator and physician William Alcott said:

But, fourthly, it is due to the nation and age to which you belong, that you fix upon a high standard of character. This work is intended for American youth. American! did I say? This word, alone, ought to call forth all of your energies, and if there be a slumbering faculty within you, arouse it to action. Never, since the creation, were the youth of any age or country so imperiously called upon to exert themselves, as those whom I now address. Never before were there so many important issues at stake. Never were such immense results depending upon a generation of men, as upon that which is now approaching the stage of action. These rising millions are destined, according to all human probability, to form by far the greatest nation that ever constituted an entire community of freemen, since the world began. To form the character of these millions involves a greater amount of responsibility, individual and collective, than any other work to which humanity has ever been called.[9]

Those words still apply today.

8

Common Sense and Wisdom

Benjamin Franklin

My father used to play with my brother and me in the yard. Mother would come out and say, "You're tearing up the grass." Dad would reply, "We are not raising grass, we're raising boys."

—Harmon Killebrew,
Baseball Hall of Fame slugger

COMMON SENSE IS DEFINED BY MERRIAM-WEBSTER AS "sound and prudent judgment based on a simple perception of the situation or facts." Aristotle believed that common sense was "an actual power of inner sensation (as opposed to the external five senses . . .) whereby the various objects of the external senses (color for sight, sound for hearing, etc.) are united and judged on a level of rationality." Others believe that common sense is more related to experience and wisdom combined with logic.

Wikipedia defines wisdom as being "a deep understanding and realization of people, things, events or situations, resulting in the ability to apply perceptions, judgments and actions in keeping with this understanding. It often requires control of one's emotional reactions so that universal principles, reason and knowledge prevail to determine one's actions. Wisdom is also the comprehension of what is true or right coupled with optimum judgment as to action."[1] Wisdom is more than just mental acuity. It's about insight and understanding—insight into how the world works, how people operate, how situations unfold and then using those insights to understand the most appropriate way to live.[2]

Perhaps the man most known throughout history for his common sense and wisdom is Benjamin Franklin.

Benjamin Franklin—The Father of Common Sense

Benjamin Franklin (1706–1790) was one of the Founding Fathers of the United States. Of all of the great men throughout history, Franklin may be one of the most underrated for his achievements. Franklin was a leading author, printer, political theorist, politician, postmaster, scientist, musician, inventor, civic activist, statesman, and diplomat. His scientific discoveries led him to be a major figure in the American Enlightenment and in physics for his discoveries and theories regarding electricity. He established both the first public lending library in America and the first fire department in Pennsylvania.

Franklin was an early campaigner for colonial unity; he spoke in London as an author and spokesman and was the first United States Ambassador to France. Franklin embodied the values of thrift, hard work, education, community spirit, and self-governing institutions.

Franklin was a successful newspaper editor and printer in Philadelphia. Franklin helped establish the University of Pennsylvania and was elected the first president of the American Philosophical Society. He became a hero in America after he spearheaded the effort to have Parliament repeal the highly unpopular Stamp

Act. He was widely admired among the French during his time as American minister to Paris. His work as the British postmaster for the colonies enabled him to set up the first national communications network. He was active in colonial and state politics, as well as national and international affairs. From 1785 to 1788, he served as governor of Pennsylvania. He was also an avid chess player and musician.

Franklin might be best known for his scientific discoveries and inventions. He developed the first lightning rod that to this day protects buildings and ships from electrical damage. Among his inventions were the first flexible urinary catheter; a carriage odometer; the glass harmonica; the iron Franklin stove (a furnace stove), allowing people to heat their homes more efficiently and safely; and mail route delivery techniques still used today. He is also credited with inventing bifocal glasses.[3]

Franklin is also famous for his publication of *Poor Richard's Almanack*. People in the colonies enjoyed them for the mixture of seasonal weather forecasts, practical household hints, puzzles, and other amusements they offered. The publication ran annually from 1732 to 1758 and was a bestseller in the colonies with print runs reaching ten thousand per year (quite a large amount for that era).

Franklin's parents were both pious Puritans and he retained a lifelong commitment to Puritan virtues and political values. Franklin's father owned a copy of the book, *Bonifacius: Essays to Do Good*, by the Puritan preacher and family friend Cotton Mather, which Franklin often cited as a key influence on his life. These Puritan values were one of Franklin's quintessentially American characteristics and helped shape the character of the nation. Franklin felt that organized religion was necessary to keep men good to their fellow men, but rarely attended religious services himself. In his autobiography he declared himself a deist but still considered himself a Christian and retained a strong faith in God as the wellspring of morality and goodness. It was Franklin who, during an impasse during the Constitutional Convention, attempted to introduce the practice of daily prayer.

When Franklin died at age eighty-four, approximately twenty thousand people attended his funeral (a huge number considering the population at the time). Franklin signed both the Declaration of Independence and the Constitution. One interesting footnote that illustrates Franklin's common sense is that upon his death he bequeathed about $4,400 each to the cities of Boston and Philadelphia to be held in trust and gather interest for two hundred years. As of 1990 the city of Philadelphia had accumulated more than two million dollars and the city of Boston almost five million.[4]

Why Common Sense and Wisdom Are Important

During times of universal deceit, telling the truth becomes a revolutionary act.

—George Orwell

Many people have asked me why it seems to have been easier to raise kids in previous generations than it is today. I think part of it is because we had a collective conscience as a culture in years past.

For instance, when I was growing up all of the programs on television promoted good, strong family values, there weren't many of what would today be considered PG-rated (much less, R-rated) movies in theaters, music lyrics were monitored to ensure that nothing vulgar was broadcast over the airwaves (or on records), there was a copy of the Ten Commandments prominently displayed in various public locations, we said the Pledge of Allegiance every day in school (and meant it), and most adults (even if they didn't follow them) believed in the basic tenets and morals of the Judeo-Christian value system.

This all unconsciously influenced children to have at least *some* foundation for life; they absorbed *some* character values through osmosis if nothing else. Just the general level of filth our children are exposed to every day today alone is enough to make raising them difficult. With no positive moral foundation to weigh this social decadence against, how can we expect children to make good judgments? Parents today often feel like they are holding up a shield against a flood, with little influence or even hope of keeping their children innocent and safe. Most segments of society do not seem to share those same values.

In the 1960s a group of social scientists developed a teaching method called Values Clarification. This was a process to determine what may or may not be right for a person in each situation. All moral "oughts" were reduced from universal, absolute values to individual, relative values. The basic premise behind this was that there are no absolute values. Values are personal to each individual and what's right for you may be wrong for someone else and vice versa. This philosophy has been largely embraced by the public education system in this country.[5]

I'm not one of those people who longs for the "good old days" and thinks we would be capable of somehow transporting our culture back to the 1950s. The changes in our culture are here to stay and we either learn to deal with them productively or throw our hands in the air and go live in a cave somewhere. Some of the changes to our culture are good and deserve to be acknowledged. We just need to use common sense in determining how to use them. Much like a gun can be a useful tool when used properly, it is also a deadly, destructive weapon in the wrong hands.

The internet gives us an incredible access to virtually any information you could possibly want. But with that access comes the danger of unlimited and unsupervised exposure to malignant topics like pornography, bomb-making, anarchist ideas, or alternative lifestyles and philosophies unheard of a few decades ago. We can also waste great amounts of time on Facebook and YouTube. It's a power like none we've ever known before. Without common sense, there is a potential for that power to be used irresponsibly. I liken it to the first people who discovered fire. They probably thought it was fantastic until the first person got badly burned or the first fire got out of control and destroyed their village. They had to learn how to handle that great power responsibly. They learned that dangers went along with all the wonderful benefits.

But common sense is a scarce commodity today. Or in the words of Voltaire, "Common sense is not so common."

When I was growing up times were much simpler. At the beginning of the school year, you typically got (or at least kids from my neighborhood got) two pair of jeans, a couple of shirts, and a pair of tennis shoes. (Chuck Taylor Converse was the only acceptable brand—Keds Red Ball Jets weren't nearly as cool. By the early 1970s Adidas had come out with blue suede sneakers that revolutionized the tennis shoe industry.) You wore the Levis (or whatever brand of jeans Montgomery Ward sold) all year until by summer they were faded and had holes in the knees. This worked out great because you just made cutoffs out of them and wore them all summer before starting over next school year. Also, by summer break your tennis shoes were worn out—but since you went barefoot all summer that didn't really matter either.

Today with the plethora of choices we have in every area of life, things are more complicated. The quicker pace of life does not often allow us to stop and use common sense or wisdom when we are making decisions. And boys especially are distracted by a variety of attractive alternatives in today's world. My wife and I were at the mall the other day. With all the bright lights, loud noises, subliminal advertising, and distracting graphics on display, I quickly felt sensory overload. Males are easily overstimulated (and attracted) by these types of environments, making them susceptible to making unwise choices. Video game designers learned this early on.

Psychologist Philip Zimbardo (famous for the Stanford prison experiment in the 1970s) gave a talk on Ted TV where he described drug addiction as "wanting more." He went on to say that boys and young men today have what he calls arousal addiction, always "wanting something different." Zimbardo cites excessive internet use, video gaming, and online porn as causes of this new addiction. By age twenty-one, boys spend ten thousand hours gaming, two-thirds of that time in isolation. The average young man watches fifty porn clips per week.

"Boys' brains are being digitally rewired in a totally new way; for change, novelty, excitement, and constant arousal," Zimbardo says. "They're totally out of sync in traditional classes, which are analog, static, and interactively passive. And they're totally out of sync in relationships, which build gradually and subtly." This is creating a generation of young men who do not connect well in traditional teaching situations and who lack social skills, especially with women.[6] So this never ending stream of stimulation is behind the growing failure of males to connect with women socially or to succeed academically. They're dropping out of life.

In addition, the movie industry contributes to this overstimulation in boys as well. Psychologist Michael Gurian states, "The film industry produces sex-and-aggression-based programming especially to lure boys . . . It's a visceral and hormone-driven approach to selling product. Boys are testosterone-based and often gravitate toward stimuli that appeal to this aggression-based hormonal system . . . The world's electronic storytellers know that the male brain tends to gravitate toward fast-moving images, aggressive stimuli, flagrant sexual possibilities, and role-model males who use aggressive force. . . . Their purpose is obviously not to help children gain moral character and clear identity; rather, it is to sell products to children and adults, to sell actors and celebrities as products, and to imprint advertising images in our minds."[7]

Clearly compulsive video gaming, watching inappropriate movies, and viewing online porn are not healthy activities for young males. But the challenge most parents face is how to stop boys from engaging in these pursuits. It used to be that a parent could put the family computer in a public area of the home and at least control some of the online activities. Now with smart phones and tablet computers, young people have internet access virtually every second of the day. Frankly, I'm not sure it's even possible, much less advisable, to try to ban your son from engaging in online activities. Perhaps a better approach is to strive for foundational development as opposed to authoritarian control. What I mean is that as our sons mature they lose their "fear" of our authority over them as parents—and frankly, they are taught this disdain for authority figures by many segments of our culture. So they will follow our wishes, our rules, and our guidance only if they know we love and care about them—*and* they respect us. In addition, they need to learn the wisdom of having the internal self-control to not engage in these types of unhealthy activities. That self-control comes from having common sense and wisdom.

How to Teach Your Son Common Sense and Wisdom

> When a father and son do spend long hours together, which some fathers and sons still do, we could say that a substance almost like food passes from the older body to the younger.
>
> —Robert Bly, *Iron John*

Unlike knowledge, wisdom comes from God. Perhaps the best way to teach boys common sense and wisdom is to mentor them (or coach them if the word *mentor* makes you uncomfortable). Benjamin Franklin had so much common sense because he studied the classics—learned from great men throughout history. Aristotle (another really smart guy—he was thought to be the last person to know everything there was to be known in his time) had so much wisdom because he had the benefit of being mentored by Plato, who had in turn been mentored by Socrates. Each succeeding generation built upon what was learned by the previous generation and pushed themselves to new revelations and higher standards. Without that previous generational wisdom that was earned through experience, we all start from scratch and have to learn the same lessons over and over again, making the same mistakes along the way.

Perhaps more boys and young men need mentoring today than at any other time in history. But with the high rates of divorce, paternal abandonment, and unwed motherhood, it's unfortunate that those who need it most are least likely to receive it, and if they do get it, are less likely to accept it. Because males are so visual, they probably need a mentor or role model even more than females do. They need to see how they are supposed to think, act, solve problems, and face life. They need to see an example of what their roles in life are and what fulfilling them looks like. Without that guidance they are left to their own devices or to the examples modeled for them by movies, TV, videos, or other young males who are adrift as well. Young males in those circumstances are especially susceptible to the influence of damaged or bad men.

Without positive mentors in life, boys are more prone to fail. Throughout history and across all cultures, data shows that boys without mentors become immoral, lost, undirected, unmotivated, and destructive. Boys need mentors and they desperately want parents to teach them what is true and how to succeed in life, although they may not be able to articulate that desire.[8]

Our culture tells males they should be ashamed of failure. But failure is how we often learn best.

In order to understand how to relate to boys it's important to understand how they are made. One of the first things we need to realize when working with boys and other males is how they process information. It is important, especially for moms, to understand that feelings are not as important to boys as they are to females. In fact, feelings to boys seem uninteresting and not of consequence. Most males are not really interested in delving into the complexities of their feelings. To most males, talk is cheap—actions speak louder than words.

The way males are created determines the way they process information. In general males have about six times more gray matter (representing information processing centers) in their brains than females. But females have about ten times the amount of white matter that represents the networking of, or connections between, those processing centers than males. Hence, females tend to be able to better "connect the dots" in their brains, and "see" sensory, memory, and emotive detail more richly and quickly than boys. Because females have a larger hippocampus, they take in more sensorial and emotive information during experiences than males. They are also better able then to access those feelings and more quickly attach words to those feelings later on. Females also tend to have verbal centers on both sides of the brain, while males only work with language in the left hemisphere of their brains. This means males not only have fewer language centers but also have less connectivity to language centers in their brains.[9]

The chemical structure of the brain also determines how boys process information. Because of the amounts and concentrations of various chemicals like serotonin, testosterone, and oxytocin, boys are less able to sit still for long periods of time than girls and tend to be more physically impulsive and aggressive. They also have a need to move up in the social pecking order in order to flourish. Additionally, when under stress, a male's brain relies more on "fight or flight" and action for stress release and response.[10]

Neuropsychiatrist Daniel Amen has done some fascinating studies regarding blood flow to the brain. Blood flow in the brain indicates its ability to process information. Amen's studies show that when males "zone out" in front of the television (or during a lengthy verbal conversation about feelings) blood flow to the brain becomes severely limited. However, when females are sitting bored with nothing to do, the blood flow to their brains continues to be

Franklin's Thirteen Virtues

Benjamin Franklin sought to cultivate his character through these thirteen virtues:

1. "Temperance. Eat not to dullness; drink not to elevation."
2. "Silence. Speak not but what may benefit others or yourself; avoid trifling conversation."
3. "Order. Let all your things have their places; let each part of your business have its time."
4. "Resolution. Resolve to perform what you ought; perform without fail what you resolve."
5. "Frugality. Make no expense but to do good to others or yourself; i.e., waste nothing."
6. "Industry. Lose no time; be always employ'd in something useful; cut off all unnecessary actions."
7. "Sincerity. Use no hurtful deceit; think innocently and justly, and, if you speak, speak accordingly."
8. "Justice. Wrong none by doing injuries, or omitting the benefits that are your duty."
9. "Moderation. Avoid extremes; forbear resenting injuries so much as you think they deserve."
10. "Cleanliness. Tolerate no uncleanliness in body, cloaths, or habitation."
11. "Tranquility. Be not disturbed at trifles, or at accidents common or unavoidable."
12. "Chastity. Rarely use venery but for health or offspring, never to dullness, weakness, or the injury of your own or another's peace or reputation."
13. "Humility. Imitate Jesus and Socrates."

quite substantial, indicating their brain is active and processing information at a high rate. So when boys are bored, their brains are "blank," taking in very little outside stimulus—in fact, they may not even be able to hear what is said to them. And unfortunately, a male's brain can shut down very quickly.[11] Keep this in mind as you have conversations with your son. It might be advantageous to have mentoring conversations while you are doing a physical activity. Males tend to process information and emotions better when they are able to move about. To sit and talk face-to-face might cause a male's brain to shut down because they are perhaps receiving more input than they can process while not being physically challenged at the same time. In addition, males tend to bond more easily and deeper when having a physical experience. Males generally do not bond by talking with each other, but when *doing* things together (sports teams, computer games, fishing, camping, playing music together, etc.).

So when talking with our sons we also need to remember that they tend to avoid vulnerability and weakness, especially when in verbal or emotional situations. Males are much less successful at verbalizing their needs, wants, desires, and feelings and hence consider themselves failures at emoting and avoid it as much as possible. Continually asking a boy how he *feels* about something is probably counterproductive and frustrating for him. Males tend to have limited stores of emotional energy and will not waste it on people they do not think care about them, or on situations where they think they might appear inadequate or incompetent (fail). Also, males tend to look for a way *out* of, to quickly *fix*, or to avoid crisis situations any way possible. Females conversely look to increase bonding relationships to work through a crisis.[12] So if your son is struggling, his natural tendency will not be to want to talk about it. But if you can quickly help him to discover a solution (not rescue him), he will be appreciative. Helping him understand how to succeed in life is one of the ways he feels loved. He will *want* to expend his limited emotional energy on those he thinks care about him.

Besides providing for and protecting our children, mentoring them may be the very definition of "parenting." When we mentor someone we intentionally teach them the things we've learned from our experiences that will help them become successful in life. But this requires us to be intentional in our instruction—to be proactive and not reactive. When we are unintentional about teaching those who look to us for guidance, a lot of the "junk" that we were raised with gets transferred to them despite our best intentions.

While it may seem most logical for fathers or other male role models to mentor boys, moms can also be effective mentors for sons provided they remember a few key factors. As a mentor for your son, establish strong and flexible boundaries for him from an early age. Males require structure in most situations in order to feel secure. You'll notice that most males are uncomfortable in unstructured environments, especially ones where emotions might get out of hand.

Boys enjoy sports for that very purpose—the rules are unwavering and everyone is subject to them. There is no ambiguity. In order to effectively mentor boys we need to give them tasks, discerning feedback, truth without ambiguity, and rituals. They also need to be challenged. They need to be challenged in order to feel safe at a deep level.[13] Without a challenge many males think, "What's the point?" Give a boy or a man a challenge and watch how they respond. They eagerly tackle it and look for ways to accomplish the task. Watch how quick men come together during a natural disaster. In working with men's ministries around the country, we've learned that men must be challenged—they must have tangible goals that they can accomplish or they will not get energized.

So give your son challenges to accomplish, then celebrate his success with rituals. Males throughout history have used rituals to acknowledge a boy or man's accomplishments. These can be simple or elaborate. For instance, challenge him to achieve a certain grade in a class or to make the school band. When he does, acknowledge it with a ritual, like going as a family for ice cream to celebrate his achievement. Another ritual might involve having breakfast out together once a week with a parent while studying a book together. Completing each challenge is acknowledged through a ritual like receiving a pin or some other trinket that signifies his accomplishment. The Boy Scouts of America are adept at this. They give merit badges during elaborate ceremonies in front of parents and families each time a boy completes a certain skill set level. They then encourage the boys to wear these badges as a sign of honor whenever they are together. At a higher level, the military does this as well, honoring men by giving ribbons and pins for accomplishments, patches for their uniforms when they achieve a higher rank, or medals when they display meritorious behavior. They too wear these proudly so that they can be honored by others for their accomplishments. The challenges and rituals that you create for your son are only limited by your imagination.

Next teach your son to take advice from the proper sources. A classic example of a young man who takes advice from the wrong people is illustrated in the Bible in 1 Kings 12. Solomon's son, Rehoboam, was being crowned as king by all the representatives of the tribes of Israel upon his father's death. The people asked him to lower the burden of taxes that his father had placed upon them. He told them to give him three days to think about it. During that time Rehoboam asked all the elders who were advisors to his father what they advised him to do. They told him in effect, "If you listen and are good to the people and lessen their burden they will serve you forever." But Rehoboam rejected their advice and asked the young men he had grown up with who were now serving him (his sycophants) what to do. What did they advise him? They told him to tell the people, "My little *finger* shall be thicker than my father's waist! And now, whereas my father put a heavy yoke on you, I will add to your yoke; my father chastised you with whips, but I will chastise you with scourges!" (1 Kings 12:10–11 NKJV).

The people of Israel soon rebelled and chose a new king. If Rehoboam had listened to the advice of sage older men he could have been a glorious leader of the people. Instead he listened to inexperienced, hotheaded young men who gave him bad advice, and he suffered the consequences. Teach your son to seek advice from people who are in the position in life that he wants to attain. Asking a poor man how to become wealthy or a man who has been divorced multiple times for advice on a happy marriage is probably counterproductive. Teach him to watch and follow other people he admires.

Next, be honest in your feedback to him on his performance. If he fails let him know openly and honestly. Do not hold back hoping to keep from hurting his feelings. Trust me, he knows when he failed or didn't give his best effort. Males develop their self-esteem not by being told they are successful but by earning that success. So be truthful when he falls short, but give him strategies that can help him overcome his failures. Most of us fail not because we want to but because we don't know how to succeed. I'm not saying you should be overly critical of him, and you should never tie his value as a person to his performance. But he appreciates honest feedback, especially if helpful advice accompanies it.

What does all this have to do with common sense and wisdom? Everything! Males who have the benefit of having loving caregivers who invest in them by pouring their life experiences into them through lessons and modeling are immensely more prepared to start out in life. Their chances of succeeding are exponentially better than a boy who has had no formal training or mentoring—and even more so if he has had *poor* modeling. The wisdom gained through someone else's past experiences means we do not have to repeat those same mistakes. The level of wisdom we approach life with determines our happiness and chances for success.

9

Vision

Thomas Jefferson

What one generation tolerates, the next generation will embrace.

—John Wesley

I predict future happiness for Americans if they can prevent the government from wasting the labors of the people under the pretense of taking care of them.

—Thomas Jefferson

VISION IS THE ABILITY TO SEE SOMETHING THAT IS, HAS been, or will be. It is the ability to see into the future. It is an unusual competence in discernment or perception; intelligent foresight. It is the ability to use your imagination to foresee or conceive of events or things that have not yet happened (future realities). Males without vision cannot be effective leaders, either in their homes or community.

One of the greatest men of vision throughout history was Thomas Jefferson.

Thomas Jefferson—Man of Vision

Thomas Jefferson (1743–1826) was an American Founding Father, the principal author of the United States Declaration of Independence, and the third president of the United States (1801–1809). He has been called the "architect of freedom."

Jefferson was an accomplished farmer, a noted gourmet, a prolific writer, inventor, and statesman. His father (who was his hero) died when Jefferson was fourteen. He escaped from his grief by immersing himself in books and music.[1]

At the beginning of the American Revolution, Jefferson served in the Continental Congress, representing Virginia. He then served as governor of Virginia (1779–1781). Later, Jefferson was a diplomat stationed in Paris as a commissioner to help negotiate commercial treaties. In May 1785, he became the United States Minister to France. He was also the first United States Secretary of State (1790–1793) during the administration of President George Washington. Elected president in 1800, he purchased the Louisiana Territory from France (1803) and sent the Lewis and Clark Expedition to explore the west (1804–1806). A leader in the Enlightenment, Jefferson spoke five languages and was deeply interested in science, religion, and philosophy. He helped found the University of Virginia in his post-presidency years. After his wife of eleven years, Martha Jefferson, died following childbirth, he remained a widower for the rest of his life. Their marriage produced six children.

Jefferson shaped the emergence of democracy in America. His concepts of democracy were rooted in the Enlightenment. He called for national self-determination and cultural uniformity. Jefferson believed that public education and a free press were essential to a democratic nation. After the Revolutionary War, Jefferson advocated restraining government via rebellion and violence when necessary in order to protect individual freedoms.

Jefferson was perhaps one of the most remarkable men in the history of the world. He started learning very early in life and never stopped.

Jefferson was heavily influenced by the English philosopher John Locke. Locke believed that the only reason for the existence of government was to protect its citizens' natural rights to "life, liberty, and property." Jefferson borrowed and modified that phrase for the Declaration of Independence.[2] Jefferson, a gifted writer, began the Declaration of Independence with these magnificent words: "We hold these truths to be self-evident, that all men are created equal, that they are endowed by their Creator with inherent and inalienable Rights, that among these are Life, Liberty and the pursuit of Happiness."

While Jefferson was inclined toward deism (belief in a God who does not intervene in human affairs), he believed strongly in the moral philosophy of Christianity and referred to himself as a "Christian" in private letters. Throughout his life Jefferson was intensely interested in theology, biblical study, and morality. He even edited a compilation of Jesus's teachings titled, *The Life and Morals of Jesus of Nazareth.*

Thomas Jefferson had the vision to design, create, and help implement a system of government that resulted in the greatest country in the history of the world with the largest number of free people enjoying the most liberty and greatest economic prosperity ever imagined—the United States of America.

Why Vision Is Important

I was bold in the pursuit of knowledge, never fearing to follow truth and reason to whatever results they led, and bearding every authority which stood in their way.

—Thomas Jefferson

A blind man once asked a wise man, "Is there anything worse than losing your eyesight?"

A Brief Outline of Jefferson's Accomplishments:

- At age 5, he began studying under his cousin's tutor. At age 9, he studied Latin, Greek, and French.
- At age 14, he studied classic literature and multiple languages.
- At 16, Jefferson entered the College of William and Mary.
- Beginning at age 19, he studied law for five years, starting under George Wythe.
- At 23, he started his own law practice.
- At 25, he was elected to the Virginia House of Burgesses.
- At 31, he wrote the widely circulated "Summary View of the Rights of British America" and retired from his law practice.
- At 32, he was a delegate to the Second Continental Congress.
- At 33, he wrote the Declaration of Independence.
- At 33, he took three years to revise Virginia's legal code and wrote a public education bill and a statute for religious freedom.
- At 36, he was elected the second governor of Virginia, succeeding Patrick Henry.
- At 40, he served in Congress for two years.   *Continued*

The wise man replied, "Yes . . . losing your vision."

One of the most important character traits a leader possesses is vision. As a culture we are losing our most valuable resource—male leadership. We have lost our vision of what role a man should play in life, and we have let young men drift along dangerously like disabled ships at sea. Cultures that allow families and communities to exist with no stable, healthy male authority and leadership eventually devolve into chaos. We are seeing the consequences of that in many urban inner city neighborhoods where with upwards of an 80 percent fatherless rate there are virtually no healthy adult male role models. Healthy masculine leadership protects the weak. It uses its influence and power to provide safe, life-giving encouragement

- At 41, he was the American Minister to France and negotiated commercial treaties with European nations along with Ben Franklin and John Adams.
- At 46, he served as the first secretary of state under George Washington.
- At 53, he served as vice president and was elected president of the American Philosophical Society.
- At 55, he drafted the Kentucky Resolutions, which became the basis of "states' rights."
- At 57, he was elected the third president of the United States.
- At 60, he obtained the Louisiana Purchase, doubling the nation's size.
- At 61, he was elected to a second term as president.
- At 65, Jefferson retired to Monticello.
- At 80, he helped President Monroe shape the Monroe Doctrine.
- At 81, he almost single-handedly created the University of Virginia and served as its first president.
- At 83, he died on the fiftieth anniversary of the signing of the Declaration of Independence, as did fellow signee John Adams.

and provision. It inspires vision in young men and women. Healthy masculinity provides security to all who are around it.

The Bible says, "Where there is no vision, the people perish" (Proverbs 29:18 KJV). Because of lack of vision (or poor vision) in the leaders today, our country and cultural value system are threatening to collapse in upon themselves.

All males, no matter their age, yearn for significance in their lives. They yearn for a battle to fight that means something. Young men run to the battlefield; not because they want to kill or be killed, but because they want to participate in a battle bigger than themselves—one that matters. They want the world to know they existed. God created them this way to make the world safe and healthy.

Separation of Church and State

As a side note, here is one item that is important to recognize. Jefferson is widely credited with the concept of the "separation of church and state," which much of our country bases policies on today. This comes from one line in a private letter he wrote to the Danbury Baptists. It reads, "Believing with you that religion is a matter which lies solely between man and his God, that he owes account to none other for his faith or his worship, that the legislative powers of government reach actions only, and not opinions, I contemplate with sovereign reverence that act of the whole American people which declared that their legislature should 'make no law respecting an establishment of religion, or prohibiting the free exercise thereof,' thus building a wall of separation between church and state." It's important to note that this phrase has repeatedly been taken out of context and used for purposes that Jefferson probably did not intend. In fact, just the opposite of how it has been utilized, Jefferson meant that the *church* should be protected from the state (government) and not vice versa. His letter was in response to the Baptists' concern that the state would infringe on their right to religious liberty.

When we teach our sons the nobility of using the awesome masculine power that God gave us to help others, we give them the ability to define their lives—we channel that natural competitiveness, aggressive nature, and yearning for significance that God gave them into healthy, life-giving outlets. The world has many battles that need to be fought by a group of men and boys banding together—things like poverty, child and domestic abuse, drug and alcohol abuse, illiteracy, sexual slavery and human trafficking, fatherlessness, and violent behavior by unhealthy men. Just like men of yore were adventurers of wild continents, explorers of untamed lands, and conquerors of the unconquerable, we need to give our young men today adventures with noble causes to live their lives for. But without a vision to inspire them many boys settle for a life lesser lived.

Boys need to hear words like *strong*, *brave*, *talented*, and *noble* in order to assimilate their duty as leaders. They need to have the adults in their lives intentionally speak affirming language that inspires and uplifts them to willingly assume the mantle that leadership imposes upon them. They need to be taught to relish the satisfaction that duty and honor bring to a man. As a culture we need to have the vision to recognize the positive attributes that healthy masculinity brings to the table and then nurture those in young men. Vision is one of those attributes.

A culture without vision is directionless. Without direction we eventually founder. A ship at sea without a vision of where it wants to go sails around in circles. Driving in a car without directions (vision) on how to get somewhere is frustrating and inefficient. Living life without a vision of who we want to be and what we want to accomplish is wasteful and maddening. Without vision in life boys are directionless and lack the ability to attain lives of significance.

How to Teach Your Son to Have Vision

> I tremble for my country when I reflect that God is just; that his justice cannot sleep forever.
>
> Thomas Jefferson

One of the greatest gifts we can give our son is to help nourish his natural gift of vision. In general, males are born with an innate sense to be able to see a bigger picture with a longer range vision of life than women. Females, due to their more nurturing nature, tend to be more focused on the immediate needs of their children and family. Often this causes their decision making to be based on instant need fulfillment, sometimes to the detriment of the larger picture. This is a good thing, and thank God females are created this way, otherwise families would never thrive and be healthy. Many times while we were raising our children my wife and I would discuss strategies to solve issues or problems that cropped up. We learned to rely upon each other's strengths. My wife had wisdom, compassion, and empathy that frequently brought us to the best way to solve situations, but sometimes I had to step back and see if her solution was in the best interest of everyone concerned in the long run.

For instance, as a loving, caring mother, my wife had a natural tendency to not want to see her children suffer. So whenever Frank was struggling with a project (like mowing the lawn) or crying in frustration because something was difficult (like completing his math homework) she had an instinctive urge to want to help (rescue) him in order to ease his burden (yes, I had to stop her from lambasting many coaches over the years). Unfortunately, this would be unhealthy for him in the long run, and I frequently had to intervene and force him to complete the task on his own. It sometimes seemed hardhearted (even to me), but today Frank has an excellent work ethic and knows the satisfaction and rewards of completing a task he starts. It will serve him well in life.

Explain to your son the natural ability (power) he has as a male to see a larger picture and to be able to see far into the future. Saying he has a special gift like this does not diminish females in any way—it empowers males to use their natural abilities. It also sets expectations in place that he feels compelled to live up to—not necessarily a bad thing. When you (as parents) make a decision based on a long-term vision of the circumstances, be sure to explain to your son how and why you are making that decision. It is important that he *see* what that process looks like as it is implemented so he can better assimilate it. For instance, oftentimes we are forced as parents to delay gratification in small ways in order to be able to afford some larger, more important purchase at a later date (e.g., we forgo eating meals out for a period of time so we can save for a family vacation).

Find opportunities to help him use his vision-developing strength. Ask him when he is making decisions what the long-term outcome of this decision might be. Ask him to envision what his future will look like and what the potential consequences of that choice might be. Help him to establish goals and strategies to move toward that outcome. Help him keep an eye on the bigger picture, future goals, and the ultimate outcome (e.g., if he has a goal to use his allowance money to buy a bicycle, he cannot spend his allowance each month on video games or candy). Then point out examples of other men using this skill so that he sees it and can visually process it. When you see it modeled in a movie be sure to point it out. Males are often very visual and often have to "see" something modeled in order to emulate it. Whenever a new theory or idea is explained to me I always want a practical, everyday example so that I can visually "see" it in my mind in order to understand it and how it applies to my world.

One thing all people yearn for is redemption. It is one reason the story of Rudolph the Red-Nosed Reindeer is cherished by young and old alike. It is the story of a young male whose perceived flaws cause him to be bullied and shunned by his peers. Until finally a powerful being (Santa Claus—representative of a parental figure) gives him a chance to use his gifts to become a hero. Santa's vision allowed him to see beyond the immediate shortcomings of the situation and envision a solution in the bigger picture. It is a powerful story of redemption that everyone can relate to. I remember as a child every time we moved or I attended a new school there were feelings of trepidation, but also a sense of anticipation and excitement at the opportunity for a fresh start—a chance to start over. A chance for redemption to be the kind of person I wanted to be. Just think, every new job is a new opportunity to succeed beyond our wildest expectations, every new school is a chance to have new friends and experience new adventures in life. When we are single, every new person we meet has the potential to explode into a lifelong love affair.

Redemption is the opportunity to right past wrongs, to correct our failures, to make amends. It makes us whole and new again, much like God's redemption of our sins.

Men with vision help others gain redemption by seeing a bigger picture (the ultimate big-picture guy is God, who sees the entire picture in ways we cannot fathom). They use their power to cast a vision of what could be. Oftentimes the mistakes or failures we have are part of the success of a bigger scheme of things. Without the vision to understand that, we are mired in our failures instead of understanding them to be part of a larger success.

Additionally, your vision as a parent, or the ability to see your son's strengths (much like Santa's with Rudolph), allows you to instill in your son a sense of fulfillment and redemption. Find opportunities for redemption for your son. I still look for chances to give my young adult children an opportunity to "start over" if they want. Look for the God-given strengths in your son and nurture those by casting a vision for him. I tell my son all the time what a good father he is going to be because of the gifts he has of being loving, patient, and dependable. My daughter knows she has untapped potential in areas such as working with special needs children, growing plants, and being a good mother because of her levelheadedness and compassion.

One way we teach our sons and cast a vision for their lives is through talking with them. But communicating verbally with boys is often a challenge. By understanding how their brains work we can develop some strategies to facilitate effective verbal communication.

To use verbal communication effectively with your son, consider using short, concise, "sound-bite-sized" sentences. Use topics that he finds interesting. Your son will want to have the simple facts presented and get to the point in a short period of time. Long-winded lectures are opportunities to shut down and daydream. Remember that timing is important. Talking to him about an important topic while he is watching a basketball game or playing a video game is counterproductive (he generally cannot focus on two things at once). Keep the discussion unemotional. Males tend to shut down when things get emotional (although teenagers may get overly emotional from time to time). Also, allow your son time to process information that is presented to him. Try telling him something and then asking him to think about it overnight so you can discuss it the next day.

By using effective communication with your son you can help him learn to make decisions using a bigger vision of life. The bigger picture is always important because that gives us a goal to shoot for and it puts smaller setbacks and discouragements into their proper perspective.

One of the things I do with the young men I mentor is to help them see the bigger picture. For instance, when they call with challenges or setbacks or concerns, I always talk to them about what I believe God's plan is for their life (it is generally a nobler vision than they might originally have had). We talk about what that future looks like and how the challenges today play into that. Do they really matter in the bigger scheme of things? Is this obstacle part of being refined and matured to be able to fulfill that vision? Is this setback actually a good thing in that it steers them back onto the right path? Those and many other questions often require the objective presence of an older person who has been through the battles and can help the young man look at the challenges he is facing with the proper perspective. That then allows him to see the bigger picture and develop vision.

10

Intellect

Leonardo da Vinci

Everyone is a genius. But if you judge a fish on its ability to climb a tree, it will live its whole life believing that it is stupid.

—Albert Einstein

We are all born ignorant, but one must work hard to remain stupid.

—Benjamin Franklin

INTELLECT REFERS TO THE MIND'S ABILITY TO COME TO correct conclusions about what is true or real, and about how to solve problems. It is the capacity for rational or intelligent thought; the capacity for knowledge. Intellect is also the power of knowing as distinguished from the power to feel. Intellect and intelligence are interrelated as intelligence is the mental ability that allows an individual to understand things. A person who uses their intelligence (thought and reason) together with critical or analytical reasoning is often referred to as an intellectual.

Many great men throughout history had intellect, but none had powerful intellect in so many diverse areas as Leonard da Vinci.

Leonardo da Vinci—Renaissance Man

Leonardo da Vinci (1452–1519) was an accomplished painter, sculptor, architect, musician, scientist, mathematician, engineer, inventor, anatomist, geologist, cartographer, botanist, and writer. Da Vinci's genius, perhaps more than that of any other figure, was the archetype of what became known as the "Renaissance man." He is thought to be perhaps the greatest painter of all time and the most diversely talented person ever to have lived.

An illegitimate son of a notary and a peasant girl, Leonardo (or "Lennie" as we Renaissance guys call him), created the *Mona Lisa* and *The Last Supper*, two of the most famous paintings of all time. Da Vinci used innovative techniques unique among his contemporaries. His detailed knowledge of anatomy, light, botany, and geology and his interest in physiognomy and the way in which humans register emotion in expression and gesture all contributed to his genius.

While not a prolific painter, da Vinci was a productive draftsman. He kept journals full of small sketches and detailed drawings of his observations. His drawing of the *Vitruvian Man* (a study of the proportions of the human body) has become a cultural icon, reproduced on items as varied as the euro and T-shirts. As an artist, he was a master of anatomy, drawing many studies of muscles, tendons, and other visible anatomical features. By dissecting corpses, da Vinci developed hundreds of pages of drawings and notes toward a treatise on anatomy, including many studies of the human skeleton as well as muscles and sinews. According to his biography, he studied the mechanical functions of the skeleton and the muscular forces that are applied to it in a manner that prefigured the modern science of biomechanics. He drew the heart and vascular system, the sex organs and other internal organs, making one of the first scientific drawings of a fetus *in utero*. He studied and drew the anatomy of many animals, dissecting cows, birds, horses, monkeys, bears, and frogs, comparing their anatomical structure with that of humans.

Da Vinci was also a prodigious inventor and was considered a technological genius. He conceptualized or envisioned modern-day devices such as a helicopter, a tank, the bicycle, concentrated solar power, and the calculator. Fascinated with flight, he also invented a hang glider. Relatively few of his designs were constructed or were even feasible during his lifetime, although several have been constructed and tested recently with positive results. He also invented precursors to items such as scissors, a primitive 33-barrel Gatling gun, a parachute, a portable bridge, and scuba gear. He made important discoveries in anatomy, civil engineering, optics, and hydrodynamics.

Leonardo's studies in science and engineering are as impressive and innovative as his artistic work. He recorded his observations in thirteen thousand pages of notes and drawings. There are compositions for paintings, studies of details and drapery, studies of faces and emotions, of animals, babies, dissections, plants, rock formations, whirlpools, war machines, helicopters, and architecture. In many cases a single topic—for example, the heart or the human fetus—is covered in detail in both words and pictures on a single sheet.

The *Codex Leicester* is the only major scientific work of Leonardo's in private hands. It is owned by Bill Gates and is displayed once a year in different cities around the world.

By all accounts, da Vinci was known as a man of high moral character and a sincere believer in Christ and the Scriptures.[1] In his last days, da Vinci sent for a priest to make his confession and to receive the Holy Sacrament. It is rumored that the king of France, Francis I, held his head as he died. Sculptor Benevenuto Cellini was quoted as saying upon da Vinci's death, "There had never been another man born in the world who knew as much as Leonardo, not so much about painting, sculpture, and architecture, as that he was a very great philosopher."[2]

Why Intellect Is Important

My blog is hardly filled with words most educated citizens would have trouble understanding. And yet a cable TV–inoculated audience wants everything dumbed down to the Kardashian level. This relentless push for less (less intelligence, less culture, less effort) is one of the boogiemen facing anyone who would mess with the rote rigor of mass schooling.

—Seth Godin, *Stop Stealing Dreams*

Males, especially young males, in our country are failing. They are rapidly falling behind in nearly all measurable educational outcomes and they are facing extreme challenges in the new roles and expectations our culture is trying to determine for them. Males are especially struggling with the core components for improving and displaying their intellect: reading and writing. When young women were behind males academically, we made national efforts to address the issue, yet our boys' failure has not garnered the same attention.

Among pre-adults, women are clearly the more successful sex academically. They graduate from college in greater numbers. Among Americans ages twenty-five to thirty-four, 34 percent of women now have a bachelor's degree but just 27 percent of men have one. A recent study at Northeastern University of the Boston Public Schools found that for the graduating class of 2007, "there were 191 black girls for every 100 boys going on to attend a four-year college or university. Among Hispanics, the ratio was 175 girls for every 100 boys; among whites, 153 for every 100."[3] And women have higher GPAs. As most professors tell it, they also have more confidence and drive. These strengths carry women through their twenties, when they are more likely than men to be in grad school and making strides in the workplace. In a number of cities, they are even outearning their brothers and boyfriends. Noted author and therapist Michael Gurian describes the challenges boys face in schools: "It is worth noting immediately that our therapy profession runs parallel to our school systems. In our schools, most teachers are female, and the majority of successful students in schools are female. Just as with our therapeutic professions, many people, even people inside the profession, do not realize how problematic our schools have become for boys."[4]

As a whole, boys today are failing miserably in school. Boys have a higher high school dropout rate than girls, are less likely to go to college than girls, and are frequently unemployed or under-employed. Part of the problem is that schools teach toward standardized testing and boys tend not to do well on standardized tests. Research shows us that the way boys learn best is a combination of natural curiosity, critical thinking, and group interaction. Generally being kinesthetic in nature, males process information when moving about (fidgeting, tapping, swinging feet in class). Because large class sizes with only one teacher prevent this kind of learning style, boys tend to "zone out" in the classroom, and when boys zone out, they underachieve. Educator Nick Szymanis says, "For boys in particular, we now recognize the need for patience with their emerging (often lagging) language skills and listening skills, their love of non-fiction and graphic novels, their kinesthetic processes and their need to physically manipulate objects while learning. Perhaps the argument is for single gender schools [as a positive solution]."[5]

Certainly part of the problem is how our culture now views masculinity in the shadow of the perpetual "gender wars" of the past several decades. Perhaps in our rush to empower girls and women we were under the mistaken assumption that we had to tear down masculinity in order to lift up femininity. Nothing could be further from the truth. It is perfectly logical to recognize that we can empower *all* people without taking from others. Good parents do it all the time—they empower *all* their children without regard to their gender. This worldview, though, has permeated all of society, including our educational system.

In his brilliant treatise, *The Abolition of Man*, C. S. Lewis addresses the struggle between a traditional worldview that recognizes the worth of objective values and natural law versus a progressive one and how it is being manifested through the educational system. In it, Lewis speculated upon the different teaching styles from years past and the more "modern" forms of public education when he said, "The difference between the old and new education will be an important one. Where the old initiated, the new merely 'conditions.' The old dealt with its pupils as grown birds deal with young birds when they teach them to fly: the new deals with them more as the poultry-keeper deals with young birds—making them thus or thus for purposes of which the birds know nothing. In a word, the old was a kind of propagation—men transmitting manhood to men: the new is merely propaganda."[6]

In their book *The Light and the Glory,* Peter Marshall and David Manuel brilliantly describe it like this, "In contrast, all totalitarian governments—whether Nazi, Communist, or Islamic—always attempt to remove the causes of faction by removing liberty and, as much as possible, freedom of thought. And through intensive indoctrination of the young, they also attempt to impose a sameness of opinion."[7]

That being said, I'm not convinced that there is a conspiracy plot in place to intentionally "dumb down" the children (particularly boys) of this country—although there is some strong evidence that certain progressive worldviews have for decades targeted three areas of the culture in order to transform it to their agenda: the media, the educational system (especially upper academia), and the suppression of religious freedom. But I do know that uneducated people (especially males) without critical thinking skills are easier to control than those who are capable of thinking for themselves. Our culture has already "dumbed" down everything to sound bites and YouTube clips. We are becoming an ignorant society.

Seth Godin describes it like this, "Even though just about everyone in the West has been through years of compulsory schooling, we see ever more belief in unfounded theories, bad financial decisions, and poor community and family planning. People's connection with science and the arts is tenuous at best, and the financial acumen of the typical consumer is pitiful. If the goal was to raise the standards for rational thought, skeptical investigation, and useful decision making, we've failed for most of our citizens."[8]

To compound that, we have become a society ruled by its emotions. The press reports misinformation about a crime and people are immediately taking to the streets in protest, rather than waiting for the criminal justice system to go through its process and find out the facts of the case. Politicians and activists then throw fuel on the fire by issuing irresponsible statements that push people's emotional hot buttons, creating even more fervor. In reality, the people (the citizens of our country) are being controlled through their emotions. They are being herded like cattle, with this strategy often being used to take the spotlight off larger, more important issues that are taking place at the same time.

Teach your sons the value of making decisions based on principles and not emotions. Our schools are not teaching children to develop critical thinking skills to determine the truth. Instead, a one-sided agenda is usually presented.

If those challenges weren't enough, we are seeing a much higher incidence in young males of brain-related problems. Although the causes of these disorders are not currently known, some research indicates that the significant increase during the past several decades of autism spectrum, ADHD, and other brain disorders in males appears to be related to the number of and types of toxins taken in by the mother during pregnancy. There may also be other factors included in this increase, including a variety of genetic factors, hormone levels and brain structure, and possibly even vaccinations. (My point is not what the causes of these problems are but the fact that we are seeing more and more of them in young males.)

How to Teach Your Son to Have Intellect

My people are destroyed for lack of knowledge.

—Hosea 4:6 NKJV

So do all these challenges mean boys are stupid or somehow inferior? Absolutely not! It just means we need to learn more about how males process and internalize information.

It's important as we work with our sons that we understand and recognize how they best learn. Again, because males are generally wired to be visual it is paramount to recognize how that affects your son's ability to learn. One quick tip to remember is that because boys do not see as well as females, they tend to need more and brighter light in order to function and process information better. Dim lighting and candles (like in a massage therapy room) tend to put me to sleep right away.

When I teach workshops for males I try to use a brightly lit room with a lot of visuals such as pictures, video clips, and hands-on items. I take a lot of breaks (about every fifty minutes) and let them move around at will if they need to while I speak. I also use object lessons to illustrate my points as often as possible. For instance, I drop a track baton on the floor to illustrate what happens when a father fails to pass along his knowledge and experience to his son. What happens when the hand-off of the baton between two members of the relay race team fails? It causes them to lose the race or be at a huge disadvantage. The same thing happens when a father drops the baton—his son either loses or has a distinct disadvantage. Only the stakes are higher—for this is the race of life. I also try to encourage verbal interaction, as this engages men more than we would anticipate. (As a side note, I have to discourage verbal interaction with female audiences, as we might have trouble getting through all of the material if I allowed them to talk at will.) Even though common knowledge says that men do not like to talk and share, I find that once you break through their initial wariness, males enjoy getting into small groups to discuss an issue or topic. Many men at retreats and conferences rate the small group interaction as their favorite part of the event.

Intelligence consists of a number of factors, including sound judgment, practical common sense, intuition, adaptability, rational thought, and analytic and cognitive abilities. Likely, the desire to continue to learn and improve oneself is an important factor in being intelligent.

In 1983, psychologist Howard Gardner developed his theory of multiple intelligences, which maintains there are many different types of "intelligences" ascribed to human beings. His original list consisted of these seven types:

1. Kinesthetic—involves body movement and physiology. Typically found in athletes and dancers.
2. Interpersonal—involves working well in groups. Typically found in salespeople, politicians, and teachers.
3. Verbal-Linguistic—involves proficiency with words and languages. Typically found in writers, public speakers, and philosophers.
4. Intrapersonal—involves being good at understanding self. Typically found in psychologists and theologians.
5. Logical-Mathematical—involves abstract reasoning and numbers. Typically found in scientists, doctors, and economists.

6. Visual-Spatial—involves hand-eye coordination and puzzle solving. Typically found in artists, engineers, and architects.
7. Musical—involves adeptness at music and rhythm. Typically found in musicians, singers, and composers.

Naturalist—involving sensitivity to nature—was added later and typically found in farmers, gardeners, naturalists, and conservationists. Since then a number of other intelligences have been suggested but excluded, including spiritual, existential, and moral intelligences.

When we see that there are different forms of intelligence, we realize that people can be gifted in one area and not another. For instance, someone like Albert Einstein, who was brilliant in Logical-Mathematical intelligence, may not have been able to speak well or relate to others successfully. We know, however, that he was anything but unintelligent.

One of the great disservices we do to males is to not encourage them to keep learning throughout their lives. Many men finish school and never pick up another book their entire lives. Most men don't attend seminars or workshops that teach them new things—especially if the workshops involve relationship skills.

With that in mind, remember that males are very spatial-visual, so when teaching and working with your son you can utilize many of the expressive arts to help him learn. For example, your teenage son may love music. Music (especially in adolescents) causes the secretion of dopamine and other chemicals in the nucleus accumbus (pleasure center) of the brain, which creates a "high."[9] That reaction fades as we age, but it's one of the reasons we so fondly remember those songs of our youth as we get older (we recollect that good feeling from our pleasure center). Musical composition is closely affiliated with mathematics. Using music to help your son understand mathematical equations can be fun and memorable.

I learned about fractions, percentages, and algebra through baseball. I loved baseball as a boy and followed my favorite professional players closely throughout the summer. I began to understand fractions by learning how to compute the batting averages, slugging percentages, and on-base percentages of the big league players I followed. Once I recognized (by chance) that a batter going two for three in a game was the same as two-thirds or .667 percent, algebra came into focus so much more clearly than the rote lessons on the chalkboard.

Visual graphics are also important to boys. It's why (depending on their age) they have posters of dinosaurs, sports stars, Star Wars figures, or bathing beauties on their bedroom walls. Graphics and photographs cause them to use both sides of their brains. In fact, the less sensitive your son is the more graphic stimulants he might need in order to access his emotional life. As Michael Gurian says, "His self-assessment abilities may very well hinge on the pictures he sees in his head more than the words he can use to understand himself."[10] Sometimes by seeing things in movies, photos, or video clips, a boy can understand himself and what he is feeling better than if he tried to sit down and parse it out by himself. Since introspection is often the key to intellectual development, it is important that your son learn as much as possible about himself.

We have to teach our sons to read more and write better. One out of four people did not read a book in 2007, with the typical person only reading four books a year.[11] Reading leads to more reading and better writing. It opens doors and grows intelligence.

Every year I help out at the local high school by evaluating senior papers. The differences between the writing skills of the females versus the skills of the males are like night and day. The females' papers, almost to a person, were exceptionally better than the males' attempts.

Want your son to read more? Try letting him read comics or graphic novels. Reading is reading—it doesn't matter if it's *War and Peace* or *Batman and Superman* (well, it probably does but not until later). Because boys are often later readers than girls, they tend to fall behind in school. This, of course, discourages them (not to mention humiliates them) and causes many males to quit trying and/or dislike reading altogether. Often boys just need extra help with reading in order to gradually catch up. They need to be encouraged in ways they enjoy, and not forced to read "what's best for them." As a boy, I used to read comics and the sports page of the newspaper "religiously" (stuff my mom referred to as "junk"). As I got into junior high, I started venturing into the library to read biographies and autobiographies on famous sports figures and adventurers. By high school I was ready to understand more complex classics such as George Orwell's *1984*, Aldous Huxley's *Brave New World*, Harper Lee's *To Kill a Mockingbird*, and J. D. Salinger's *Catcher in the Rye*. I'm pretty sure my parents and teachers never thought I would be a writer for a living but in retrospect it was very good training for this kind of career. It instilled in me a love of reading that has served me well throughout life. Had I been forced to suffer through Plato's dialogues as a twelve-year-old, I'm almost positive I would not be a reader today.

Drawing is an effective tool for teaching some boys. Many boys or men are intimidated by writing words on paper, possibly having had bad experiences in school. Drawing also helps males use both sides of their brain. You'll notice many boys draw in their notebooks at school. They draw warrior figures, cars, horses, and a plethora of other things. One form of therapy successfully uses drawing to help males express their internal language and emotions that they might not otherwise be able to speak. You might learn some interesting things about your son by encouraging him to draw.

Video games are popular with most boys today. Due to the visual nature of the games, boys derive a great deal of satisfaction from the visual-graphic-spatial aspect involved with playing them. All too often they can become addicting if not played responsibly. Boys receive a "wash" of dopamine and great psychological rewards from playing these games. Much like with gambling or even drug use, the effects can be addicting.

Help your son to recognize his learning style or conscious thought language (modality). Many boys are kinesthetic learners (like muscle memory) and require bodily experiences to process information. I need to physically walk through and experience something before I can truly understand it. Many athletes I have worked with require walking through a play instead of just having it drawn on a clipboard before they understand what is expected of them.

Other people are auditory learners. They learn best by *hearing* another's words or music. Many others are visual learners. They need to *see* something in their minds in order to process it. Finally some people learn best by verbal thought. They have an inner speech that helps them learn best. I try to incorporate all of these learning styles in each of the seminars or workshops I deliver. This not only reaches people at all learning levels and styles, but each style helps to reinforce the point I am trying to teach.

Perhaps one of the most important skills a person (especially a leader) can develop is the ability to think through an issue and discern the important aspects of that issue while not being distracted by the parts that are of no consequence. Your son needs to learn to distinguish between fact and opinion. He needs to understand how to compare and contrast information. Too often important issues are clouded by emotions or hyperbole. In addition, with today's technology it is easy to establish something on the internet that quickly becomes assumed as fact. As an example, books, magazines, or newspapers printing "facts" that are not backed up by well-rounded research with cited sources are really just printing their opinion. Television news programs are notorious for this today.

If you want your son to be someone who is not easily swayed by political agendas, misinformation, or opinions, he needs to develop good critical thinking skills.

How do you help a boy develop critical thinking skills that are crucial for him to learn in order to develop into a good problem solver? There are some basic ways to develop critical thinking skills—but I encourage you to be creative and intentional in your approach. First, as difficult as it may be, allow your son to argue or debate issues that do not relate to emergency circumstances. He is developing the process of understanding how to look at an issue critically from different sides. You'll notice that sometimes, if you agree with him, he may even switch his opinion in the middle of an argument and argue the other side. Also, while it may be annoying, allow him to ask a lot of questions. That shows he has an active mind and is searching for information and knowledge. (Or else he's just being a pain, but you can hope for the former.)

Encourage him to think logically. Use concrete examples whenever possible that lead to logical conclusions. For instance, someone might try to argue against the validity of gravity, but they will still hit the ground if they jump off a building. Logic takes the emotion out of an argument. Also, allow him to think through an issue or problem—do not rush in and give him the answer right away. It takes the male brain longer than the female brain to process information.[12] Answer all of his "why" questions, even if they become annoying. Teach him how to find knowledge and to seek information.

Think out loud in front of him—that way he can see and hear how you puzzle through the process of solving a problem. Finally, challenge him to look at both sides of an issue. If you only get one opinion on a subject, you cannot truly understand it. One of the great lessons I have learned in life is that you cannot understand another's pain if you have not walked in their shoes. This will serve him well later in life when he has a wife and children and issues are seldom simply black and white but are complicated shades of gray.

Teach your son *how* to learn, not how to memorize facts. Teach him to be curious and excited about learning new things. Encourage him to dream and then seek out information about his dreams from all different sources. Motivate and push him. Teach him that information and education are power.

Last, teach your son that it is manly to be intelligent.

11

Compassion and Empathy

George Müller

How far you go in life depends on your being tender with the young, compassionate with the aged, sympathetic with the striving and tolerant of the weak and strong. Because someday in your life you will have been all of these.

—George Washington Carver

COMPASSION IS THE ABILITY TO FEEL SORROW FOR ANother's misfortune and want to alleviate it. It is having the emotional capacity to be conscious of another's distress. It is a shared sense of suffering.

Empathy is the ability to put yourself in another's shoes. It is being able to imagine what another is going through and feeling. It involves being capable of understanding, being aware of, being sensitive to, and experiencing the feelings, thoughts, and experiences of another without having those feelings, thoughts, and experiences being communicated to you. Empathy is the first step to having compassion.

I struggled to find a great man whose main character trait was compassion. Many great men had compassion but it did not seem to be an overriding trait in their life. The male gender does not appear to produce (or maybe value) their own versions of Mother Teresa, Florence Nightingale, or Clara Barton. Men like Albert Schweitzer and David Livingstone both came to mind. But then my brilliant editor suggested a man I had never heard of before. When I read about his accomplishments, I was blown away!

George Müller—The Man Who Cared

George Müller (1805–1898) was a Christian evangelist and orphanage director in Bristol, England. It is estimated that his orphanages cared for over 10,024 orphans during his lifetime. He also established 117 schools, which offered Christian education to over 120,000 children.

Despite an inauspicious start (he was stealing, drinking, gambling, and a known liar by age ten), Müller became a Christian when his father sent him to school and a friend invited him to a prayer meeting. That night he asked God for salvation and immediately stopped drinking, lying, and stealing. Hoping to become a missionary, he started preaching regularly in nearby churches.

After becoming seriously ill, Müller moved to Bristol and started the Scriptural Knowledge Institution for Home and Abroad, with the goal of aiding Christian schools and missionaries; distributing Bibles and Christian tracts; and providing day schools, Sunday schools and adult schools. Within a year there were five day schools in operation—two for boys and three for girls. This project (and all of Müller's projects) never received any government support and only accepted unsolicited gifts. By the time of Müller's death this organization had received and disbursed £1,381,171 (approximately $2,718,844 USD)—around £90 million in today's terms—primarily using the money for supporting the orphanages. They also distributed about 285,407 Bibles, 1,459,506 New Testaments, and 244,351 other religious texts, which were translated into twenty different languages. The money was also used to support other "faith missionaries" around the world. Their work continues to this day.

Müller's orphanage work began in 1836 in his own home, accommodating approximately thirty girls. He quickly started three more homes that took in 130 children. By 1870 they were caring for 1,722 children in five facilities. Müller was known for the compassionate care and the superb education he provided each child.

Müller never asked for financial support, nor did he go into debt, even though the five homes cost over £100,000 to build. Accounting records were scrupulously kept and made available for scrutiny throughout his lifetime.

Müller was a huge believer in the power of prayer. Many times, he received unsolicited food donations just hours before they were needed. On one well-documented occasion, when all the children were sitting at the table, they gave thanks for breakfast, even though there was nothing to eat in the house. As they finished praying, the baker knocked on the door with sufficient fresh bread to feed everyone, and the milkman gave them plenty of fresh milk because his cart broke down in front of the orphanage.

Each morning the orphans spent time in prayer and reading the Bible. Every child who left the orphanage received a Bible and a tin trunk with two changes of clothing. The children were well dressed and well educated. School inspectors were hired to maintain high educational standards. Müller went to great lengths to find good employment for his charges after they left his homes. Nearby factories and mines claimed they were unable to obtain enough workers because of his efforts in securing positions for the children old enough to leave the orphanage.

Müller prayed about everything and expected that each prayer would be answered. Several well-known stories illustrate his faith and the rewards of that faith.

One example occurred when one of the orphan house's boilers stopped working. The boiler was bricked up and the weather was steadily worsening. Müller quickly prayed for two things; firstly that the workers he had hired would take it upon themselves to work throughout the night, and secondly that the bad weather would hold off. On the day before the work was due to commence, the weather was bitterly cold. But on the morning before the workmen arrived, a southerly wind began to blow and it was so mild that no fires were needed to heat the buildings. That evening, when the foreman of the contracted company attended the site to see how he might speed things along, the team leader stated that they would prefer to work through the night instead of going home. The job was done well before bad weather arrived.

During another winter, strong gales caused considerable damage in the area and over twenty holes were opened in the roofs of the orphanages. Around twenty windows were also broken. The glazier and slater normally employed had already committed their staff to other work so nothing could be done until the following Monday. Had the winds and heavy rains continued, the damage to the orphanage would have been substantial. After much prayer, the wind stopped in the afternoon and no rain fell until Wednesday, by which time most of the damage had been repaired.

Another story illustrating Müller praying for God's intervention occurred on the SS *Sardinian* in August 1877 while crossing the Atlantic. His ship ran into thick fog. Müller told the captain that he needed to be in Quebec by the following afternoon, but Captain Joseph E. Dutton said that he was slowing the ship down for safety. Müller would miss his appointment. Müller asked to use the chartroom to pray for the lifting of the fog. The captain claimed prayer would be a waste of time but followed him below decks. When the two men went back to the bridge, they found the fog had lifted. The captain became a Christian shortly afterwards and later became known as "Holy Joe."

Müller spent hours in daily prayer and Bible reading. It was his practice, in later years, to read through the entire Bible four times a year.

Today, the George Müller Charitable Trust still maintains the key principle of seeking money through prayer alone, and actively shuns fund-raising activities. The charity works together with local churches in the area to enable them to reach out and care for their communities. They especially target children and young people, and families with physical, emotional, social, or spiritual needs. They also encourage giving to missions and relief efforts around the world.

Müller's compassion and empathy for others lives on today. It is impossible to count how many people's lives have been saved, changed, salvaged, or helped through his efforts; but I would estimate it has to be in the millions. God took one man with a heart of compassion and used him to touch the world in ways that still echo across time.

Why Compassion and Empathy Are Important

Compassion and empathy are the essence of a man's soul. It is from the soul that all goodness springs: love, mercy, charity, forgiveness, respect, and humility, among others. These are the traits that remain after the body dies and decomposes. These are also the traits that most often touch the lives of others in ways that are remembered.

Boys need to learn compassion for others or they become self-centered and self-focused. When that happens, other people in their lives suffer. Without empathy and compassion boys do not become whole men. They are out of balance, never having the softer traits (gentleness, caring, loving) to knock the rough edges off their harder core traits (aggression, ambition, selfishness).

Grecian philosophy likened the governing or reasoning ability of man as being represented by the head or brain, the protective and virtuous spirit of man as the chest, and the stomach as being the more base appetites of a man. C. S. Lewis purported that a man's head (intellect) rules his belly (base instincts, lusts, and desires) *only* through his chest (heart) containing traits such as magnanimity and sentiment, which are indispensable as a liaison between "cerebral man and visceral man." As he said, "It may even be that it is by this middle element that man is man: for by his intellect [alone] he is mere spirit and by his appetite mere animal."[1]

Boys who do not learn to have compassion and empathy seldom develop the ability to understand and love others, including themselves.

How to Teach Your Son Compassion and Empathy

Mothers are key factors in teaching boys about compassion and empathy. A mother's unconditional style of love helps boys—merely through her example—understand what it means to have compassion and empathy for others. A woman was created to be more nurturing than a man (in general). A mom has the capability of being empathetic whenever anyone is feeling bad, comforting when they are wounded, and healing when they are in pain. She is more often than not caring, kind, thoughtful, gentle, compassionate, loving, and sensitive. She feels compelled to make sure the children are safe, fed properly, washed, and clean, with all their needs met. Her presence helps children thrive and grow like vigorous stalks of corn in fertile soil. Her nurturing instincts bring vitality to family life. Her healing touch cures everything from scraped knees to bruised egos. Her gentle compassion soothes even the most horrendous betrayal. Women love to encourage and support other people in their search for meaning in their lives. They love to share their life experiences with one another. They like to help others with their problems.

Dad, make sure you value and respect your wife's loving, nurturing nature in front of the children. Make sure they understand how important it is for the family to thrive and grow. These are powerful lessons your son needs to learn if he is to become a "whole" man.

Surprisingly, death seems to be one of the more effective lenses through which we can teach boys about compassion and empathy. One activity that turns out to be very healthy in the emotional development of boys is hunting. Societal wisdom might suggest that killing an animal (hunting) would breed violence and cruelty in males. But research suggests just the opposite is true. Hunting, in fact, actually develops respect and reverence for life and other universal virtues in males such as generosity, fortitude, respect, patience, humility, and courage. I remember the first deer I killed—the experience really sunk several lessons into me: (1) how fragile life actually is, and (2) that guns were not toys but highly destructive tools not to be used lightly. These are lessons I've carried my entire life.

According to family therapist and bestselling author Michael Gurian, hunting paradoxically makes males more empathetic and develops responsibility, fairness, and compassion. Besides war, it is the most powerful way for males to learn these virtues. Gurian contends that healthy, safe hunting under the guidance and training of mentors actually produces a holistic experience that creates less violence in young males. In contrast, the one-dimensional experience of violent video games that do not show the real-life consequences of life and death instead generates more violence in males. Hunting helps develop a sense of self-mastery and impulse control in males that contributes to a healthy self-esteem. As Gurian says, "Hunting has proven to be across the spectrum—especially in those males we think of as violent, criminal males—as having great results in teaching those guys to hunt and getting them reoriented toward things they couldn't get in the inner city, so they even see a gun in a new way by learning to use it to hunt. It's why we are having success at places like Idaho Youth ranch. Places where boys are hardened criminals, but they'll kill an animal and hold it and weep."[2]

Dr. Randall Eaton is an award-winning author and behavioral scientist with an international reputation in wildlife conservation. During a recent conversation I had with Dr. Eaton, he told me,

> Hunting is one of the most transformative experiences a boy can have. Women are adapted to *bring* life into the world, but men are adapted to *take* life in order to support or protect life. I conducted thousands of surveys on older men and asked them to choose the life experience that most opened their hearts and engendered compassion in them. It was not becoming a parent, which was extremely high for women who had birthed a baby, nor was it teaching young people, nor the death of a loved one or beloved pet, but it was "taking the life of an animal."

According to Dr. Eaton, hunting makes men more compassionate and more peaceful. As he says, "Hunting and killing are as fundamental to male development as birthing and infant care are to women. . . . Men take life to support life, and the kill itself is the event that engenders compassion, respect for life, and the moral responsibility to protect it."[3] In his surveys of men who had hunted all their lives, the men overwhelmingly selected three universal virtues that they acquired from hunting: inner peace, patience, and humility. He cites Jimmy Carter and Nelson Mandela as just two of many famous men who are examples of both exemplary hunters and peacemakers.[4]

Another effective way to teach boys about compassion and empathy is through pets. Having them take care of and be responsible for nurturing, raising, and providing for an animal not only teaches them emotional maturity but also prepares them to lead and provide for a family. Since boys and dogs go together like bacon and burgers, it's no surprise that one of my most powerful lessons about compassion came through a dog.

The first time I saw Old Lucky Dog, she came loping across the manufacturing plant wearing a slipshod, homemade, foam rubber collar someone had titled "Cecil." I took an instant liking to this clumsy, barrel-chested mongrel puppy. Discovering her to be a stray, and having been looking for a handsome pup to call my own, I decided to claim her. I quickly phoned my wife to notify her I was bringing home a cute little puppy. She was not impressed when I wrestled a 30-pound mutt through the front door. Thinking this dog fortunate to have been rescued by such a good master from the grasp of a savage winter storm, I decided to call her Lucky. I was soon to learn that destiny had already christened her with that apropos appellation.

At first glance Lucky appeared to resemble a small female moose. She was a short-haired, tawny-yellow, German shepherd-looking hound, powerful through the chest and shoulders, with semblance to an Australian dingo. With oversized ears (which pricked straight up to their fullest glory whenever the words "walk," "car," or "biscuit" were murmured) and a long, brown muzzle attached to a hard, lumpy skull, she aptly acquired the nickname "Moose." Other nomenclatures she's been called include floppy-eared, good-for-nothing, chicken thievin', mud-wallowing, and yeller dog—usually while I was chasing her around the yard with a rolled-up newspaper.

As she grew into an eighty-pound cur, some of Old Lucky Dog's favorite pastimes included chasing pheasants in the vacant fields around our home, being visited by neighbor kids for walks or tea parties in her doghouse, chasing her tail for hours on end, and wildly snorting and shaking as she hunted rabbits in her sleep. To the amazement of anyone who ever met her, Lucky Dog would do absolutely anything for a biscuit. We taught her to roll over, sit up, moan, howl, stand on her hind legs and walk backward, and even flop down and play dead if you shot her with your finger (always with one eye open looking for her biscuit). She ran around with a grin on her face most of the time and was blessed with an almost human sense of humor. One Christmas, we harnessed her to a sled and tied cardboard antlers to her head to pull the children around the neighborhood. Another time we had a family portrait taken with everyone wearing nose glasses, including Old Lucky Dog.

When we purchased our new home, I learned an interesting fact about our canine friends. They have a propensity to "dogmatize" a yard. Our beautiful Norman Rockwell landscape was almost instantly turned into a quagmire, a virtual swamp complete with dog paths, steaming smelly mounds, trashed flower beds, and holes—lots of holes. Being a known digger, Lucky excavated large quantities of earth under the guise of keeping the property free of moles. She was even kind enough to leave one on the patio one morning to justify her actions. Another interesting trait about "Moose" was her inability to bark like a normal dog. Consequently, at the drop of a hat, she would break into an uncontrollable, long, drawn out, piercing, hoarse fit of howling. I attributed this to either lack of vocal cords or an underdeveloped brain stem.

Lucky was fond of adventure and was a master escape artist from our fenced backyard. Learning of the high fees we paid several times to bail her out of the dog pound prompted my brother to remark that Lucky was her last name—Darn was her first name as far as he was concerned. Old Lucky Dog did lead a charmed life. She was once hit by a car (luckily for her head-on), and generally turned up like a bad penny no matter how much she was encouraged to find a new residence. She was found (and returned by an ex-neighbor who thought he was doing us a favor) at a distant grocery store, stepping on the electric door opener, greeting customers and escorting them to their cars (most likely in hopes of bagging a biscuit). She was found "playing" in a busy intersection ten miles away, again returned by a Good Samaritan after I was dumb enough to forget to remove her nametag from around her neck. Even after being spayed, she was undaunted, and frisked out alongside the attendant, piddling all the way down the hall in ecstasy of seeing her family again.

Though undoubtedly a fine specimen of doghood and extremely intelligent in matters pertaining to her own self-gratification, she could truly have been considered "lucky" in every sense of the word. Her dumb-luck philosophical approach to life, though cute to anyone spending short periods of time with her, was often frustrating and the cause of great aggravation. But she was an addictive, acquired taste, much beloved by the family.

One day during her prime, Old Lucky Dog started having seizures. We discovered that she had epilepsy and were directed to give her phenobarbital to control her seizures. As she developed a tolerance to the drug, even larger doses became less effective and sapped her personality. One day I found Old Lucky Dog during a rainstorm, collapsed and drowning in the mud, unable to stand up—a shell of her former self—and knew her luck had run out. Taking her to the pound and staying with her while she was put to sleep was truly one of the hardest things I had endured to that point in life. Over the years I've liked to think that Old Lucky Dog is having fun in dog heaven, running like the wind, ears flopping, chasing all those rabbits and pheasants, and eating as many biscuits as her belly will hold. I still miss Old Lucky Dog.

The scene from the movie *Old Yeller* comes to mind when the boy, Travis, is forced to shoot Old Yeller after he becomes infected from fighting off an attack by a rabid wolf. If you don't cry out of compassion and empathy during that scene, you don't have a heart.

So, am I saying if you want to teach your son empathy and compassion get him a dog? Yeah, maybe I am—a boy needs a dog. One of the great lessons (and blessings) in life is to have enjoyed the unconditional loyalty and companionship of a good dog.

12

Warrior-Poet

David

Strength and honor!
—Maximus Decimus
Meridius, *Gladiator*

THE WARRIOR-POET IS THE ANCIENT TRADITION OF
dedication to developing the body and the mind equally as
one, using each to guide the other. The warrior-poet is often
a spiritual warrior as well. They live their life by higher standards
than do average men.

Many of the current special forces warriors of the US military
branches might be considered modern-day warrior-poets. They are
highly trained and skilled in all areas of warfare, yet many have advanced degrees in subjects such as philosophy, literature, engineering,
or even poetry. They are all the more effective because their minds and
bodies are highly developed to function as one. They are no longer
just programmed killing machines, but highly intelligent and adaptive "whole" men, trained to use their minds as well as their bodies.

King David—The Warrior-Poet

There may have been no man more rugged, more masculine, or a more powerful leader in the entire Bible than David. David started being passionate, courageous, and spiritually faithful very early in life. One time when he was a young teenage shepherd boy, a bear made off with one of his flock. David tracked it down and killed it with just his bare hands to get his sheep back! Another time he did the same with a lion! Think about that, killing bears and lions without a weapon! Then, as if those accomplishments weren't enough, while still a teenager, he killed a heavily armed giant with a bad attitude, using just a sling and a rock while all the rest of the army of grown men and battle-hardened warriors trembled with fear in a ditch behind him. David's unique training probably had him spending great amounts of time by himself in the fields, talking with God and practicing his sling. Even before David battled with Goliath, God had anointed him to be the next king of Israel.

David's battle with Goliath is described in 1 Samuel 17. I think it's important to put this confrontation into perspective so we can put ourselves in David's shoes. This encounter was so much more than just a battle between two soldiers.

At the time, David was just a teenager, described as slight of build, fair-skinned, and not very tall. While bringing lunch to the battlefield for his brothers, David heard Goliath insulting God, laughing and taunting the soldiers and the God of Israel. He was perplexed and angry that no one was doing anything about it, and so he confidently volunteered to handle Goliath himself. David probably figured he'd already killed a lion and a bear with his bare hands—how tough could a measly giant be? David perhaps knew even then that the Lord's Spirit was on him and with that confidence likely did not fear a mere mortal man.

Goliath was the mightiest warrior of the entire Philistine army. The Israeli army was deathly afraid of him as every day he strode forward from the enemy camp and hurled insults at the Israelites and their God. He was reported to be six cubits and a span tall. A cubit is approximately eighteen inches in length and a span is about nine inches, which would have made Goliath a towering nine foot nine (about three feet taller than the average NBA power forward). In order to wear the gear the Bible describes, he had to be heavily muscled, so I think it's fair to say he probably weighed at least in the neighborhood of five hundred pounds.

Goliath is described as wearing a coat of armor (plates of bronze sewn overlapping on a leather coat), which weighed five thousand shekels, or about 125 pounds. He carried a bronze javelin, the staff of which was like a weaver's beam—between 2.5 to three inches in diameter. I don't know how long it was but it had to be huge if the diameter was as big around as the head of a baseball bat. Let's estimate for the sake of speculation that an average spear is one inch in diameter and approximately six to eight feet long. That would, by extrapolation, make Goliath's spear about fifteen to twenty feet long. If it was made of solid bronze, it would weigh at minimum about 270 pounds at 2.5 inches in diameter, and about 345 pounds if three inches in diameter, which would seem excessively heavy even for a behemoth like Goliath.[1]

An Olympic javelin today is approximately one inch in diameter, weighs about 800 grams (1.76 pounds), and is about 2.6 meters long (8.5 feet). So even if Goliath's spear was made of wood, I estimated the weight of an average wooden pole one inch by 8.5 foot long and came up with about four pounds. (I readily admit my math skills are rusty—any engineers out there please feel free to correct me if I'm wrong.) Since Goliath's javelin was about three times as thick and twice as long as that model, I estimate that a wooden spear probably weighed in the range of 22 to 26 pounds. Attached to this pole was an iron spearhead weighing 600 shekels or about 17 pounds for a total weight of maybe 43 pounds—a pretty hefty chunk of weight to carry around and throw. He also wore a bronze helmet on his head, bronze armor (greaves) on his legs, and had a shield-bearer in front of him. He was a veritable war machine—bigger and more powerful than any three men combined.

As scrawny little David approached the field of battle with just his shepherd's staff and sling, Goliath looked down his nose at him and sneered with contempt, "Am I a dog, that you come at me with sticks? . . . Come here [boy] and I'll give your flesh to the birds of the air and the beasts of the field!" (1 Samuel 17:43–44 NIV 1984).

Then David, in a classic line, responded with complete confidence, "You come against me with sword and spear and javelin. But I come against you in the name of the LORD Almighty, the God of the armies of Israel, whom you have defied. This day the LORD will deliver you into my hands, and I'll strike you down and cut off your head" (1 Samuel 17:45–46 NIV 1984). Enraged, Goliath charged. It must have been like being charged by an angry bull elephant, ground thundering and dust flying. But David, having calmly picked up five smooth stones, ran forward and slung one from his sling like a missile that struck Goliath and embedded itself in his forehead, dropping him like a dirty shirt. David then walked over, picked up Goliath's huge sword, and hacked off his giant head, holding it up and taunting the enemy army with it. The entire Philistine army turned tail and ran.

After that, Saul made David a commander of his armies. David was an awesome warrior—his faith in God inspired him to attempt feats that average men were scared to even think about. One time Saul offered him his daughter Michal in marriage if he were to bring him more than two hundred foreskins of the Philistines. David did it and married Saul's daughter (a tragic story—read it sometime). Saul eventually became increasingly more paranoid and jealous of David's fame and started trying to kill him.

But David was such a strong leader he inspired even Jonathan, the son of King Saul and a mighty warrior himself, to love him more than a brother. Jonathan looked up to David so much that

David's Mighty Men

The book of 2 Samuel, chapter 23, has always cranked something on the inside of me. Here is where we read about David's Mighty Men:

David's Three Men

⁸These are the names of David's mightiest warriors. The first was Jashobeam the Hacmonite, who was leader of the Three—the three mightiest warriors among David's men. He once used his spear to kill 800 enemy warriors in a single battle.
⁹Next in rank among the Three was Eleazar son of Dodai, a descendant of Ahoah. Once Eleazar and David stood together against the Philistines when the entire Israelite army had fled. ¹⁰He killed Philistines until his hand was too tired to lift his sword, and the LORD gave him a great victory that day. The rest of the army did not return until it was time to collect the plunder!
¹¹Next in rank was Shammah son of Agee from Harar. One time the Philistines gathered at Lehi and attacked the Israelites in a field full of lentils. The Israelite army fled, ¹²but Shammah held his ground in the middle of the field and beat back the Philistines. So the LORD brought about a great victory.

David's Thirty Mighty Men

¹⁸Abishai son of Zeruiah, the brother of Joab, was the leader of the Thirty. He once used his spear to kill 300 enemy warriors in a single battle. It was by such feats that he became as famous as the Three. ¹⁹Abishai was the most famous of the Thirty and was their commander, though he was not one of the Three.
²⁰There was also Benaiah son of Jehoiada, a valiant warrior from Kabzeel. He did many heroic deeds, which included killing two champions of Moab. Another time, on a snowy day, he chased a lion down into a pit and killed it. ²¹Once, armed only with a club, he killed a great Egyptian warrior who was armed with a spear. Benaiah wrenched the spear from the Egyptian's hand and killed him with it. ²²Deeds like these made Benaiah as famous as the Three mightiest warriors. ²³He was more honored than the other members of the Thirty, though he was not one of the Three. And David made him captain of his bodyguard. (NLT)

he willingly gave over his birthright to the throne of the land in order that David could be king. He even risked his life to help save David the many times when his father tried to kill him. Eventually, David was banished and forced to run and hide to save his life.

David's leadership inspired men to follow him unto death. And these weren't just any men—they were the bravest and fiercest warriors in the whole kingdom. David had an inner circle of the mightiest warriors in the kingdom called his Mighty Men. The leaders of that group included the top three warriors in the entire land; one of them had even killed eight hundred men in a single battle! These men were so inspired by David's leadership that they followed him everywhere, even living in caves when King Saul put a bounty on his head. David inspired such loyalty in his men that three of the Mighty Men snuck into the enemy army's camp just to get him a drink of water when he complained of being thirsty.

But for all his skill as a warrior, David was also an accomplished poet (he wrote many of the psalms in the book of Psalms), a song-writer, and a musician. He also liked to dance in public—even scantily clad—to worship God. He was a noted musician who had soothed Saul with music during his periods of insanity. He was educated and could read and write when many men (especially warriors) couldn't. This gave him a distinct advantage over his less-educated opponents.

David was known as a warrior-poet. The warrior-poets followed the ancient tradition of dedication to developing the body and the mind as one. They were defined by their dedication to their crafts of warfare and intellectual study and reflection. The warrior-poet is also a spiritual warrior, existing to balance the cruel realities of the earth, while living by the standards of the heavens.

David was a man's man. And yet he was flawed. He made many mistakes. He wasn't necessarily a good husband. He committed adultery and then had the woman's husband (a good and loyal man) killed by sending him into a battle that he could not survive. He wasn't necessarily the best father around. One of his sons tried to overthrow him as king and have him killed. He wasn't the holiest man to walk the face of the earth. He was often scared and frustrated with God. But David had great faith in God and cried out to him in his fear, pain, frustration, anguish, and joy. God called him a "man after my own heart" (Acts 13:22 NIV). David shows us that even if we are imperfect men, reliance on God can make us men who can change history.

Why Being a Warrior-Poet Is Important

Most of us males have the blood of warriors coursing through our veins. We've just forgotten the responsibility that comes with that honor. In order to lead balanced lives, though, we need to be both strong and sensitive. We need to develop our bodies and physical skills while developing our minds as well. Too much emphasis on strength and a man can be arrogant, brutal, and crude. He leads by fear and intimidation. He is less a man because he is uneducated and too rough by not having the arts influence his character. He lacks compassion and empathy, never appreciating beauty or grace.

Too much sensitivity and a man can become ineffective as a leader, becoming paralyzed by trying to be too fair; he becomes indecisive. He is not respected because he cannot make tough decisions and stick to them when necessary. He allows others to steal or usurp his natural leadership role from him. He compromises his values when trying to appease everyone. He is too sensitive to criticism and afraid to speak the truth in his effort to be liked by all. He is afraid of his responsibilities and swayed by emotional arguments from others. He is less a man, which frustrates him and causes him to feel unfulfilled. Oftentimes his wife loses respect for him, which diminishes her love.

A man, a leader, needs both aspects—heart and head—to be effective. Men with both areas developed become confident as leaders. They step forward and rise to challenges while others wait to see what will happen. These men strive for personal improvement throughout their lives. They read books, attend workshops and seminars, and continue to educate themselves throughout their lives. They also develop their artistic sides. Perhaps they visit museums or take up painting or sculpting. They learn to play musical instruments or sing in choirs or music groups. Maybe they take dancing lessons with their wives or develop a passion for photography.

It is easier for others to follow a confident man. Lack of self-confidence afflicts many people. It keeps men from trying things they'd like to do, or should do, but fear they will fail or appear inadequate. It keeps males from stretching and reaching for the highest challenges.

When men develop not only their bodies but the artistic and intellectual sides of their personalities as well they naturally attract followers and influence people. They become natural leaders of their families and communities.

When I speak to groups of men the first thing I usually do is tell them how important they are—that they *matter* in the world. Men are so downtrodden today that they believe the myth that has been foisted upon them—that they are unnecessary. It's a message they get from many different sources every day. I tell them to look around at the building they are in. I ask, "Who built this structure?" The answer is, "Men did." I ask them who built the homes they live in, the churches they attend, the roads they drive on? Who created most of the world's greatest inventions and conquered and civilized the planet? Who explored and conquered the untamed parts of the planet? Who made it safe in America for women and children to live lives without threat of death, disease, or poverty? The answer to all those questions is again, for the most part, men. You can literally watch these men's countenance change as I speak; their heads raise, their chests puff out a bit, and they gain a higher degree of self-respect.

To speak the truth about men's accomplishments is not to minimize the contribution or accomplishments of women, it's merely stating the obvious (which is politically incorrect in today's environment).

Perhaps because our culture has somehow minimized the majestic qualities of manhood, our boys today seem a bit softer, perhaps more feminized, than in the past. They seem a bit gun-shy—with a deer in the headlights look about them. They stay in puberty longer and delay launching into manhood later than their predecessors. (Why become a man when being a man is bad?) They tend to exhibit more female-associated traits such as passivity and indecisiveness. Young men today even have lower sperm counts than men in the past. Sperm counts in males of developed countries have been dropping for the past fifty years.[2] Others, perhaps because they have been caused to be ashamed of being a male, overcompensate by acting out in dramatic caricatures of manhood—they are overly macho, violent, and sexually promiscuous.

Young men today also have a certain amount of repressed anger. This may contribute to the seeming increase in bullying in schools, but also in a more escalated *level* or *degree* of violence among young males. This is possibly caused by not allowing young males to solve their social issues as they have for thousands of years—on their own. In the past when two young males disagreed about something, they went to the playground and tussled around until one or the other acceded—generally they both just got too tired to continue and quit. They then shook hands and forgot about it. In fact, many boys I fought with went on to become my good friends. Today, however, with adult interference, boys are not allowed to solve their own problems. They are taught that any kind of aggression or (gasp) violence is bad. So they are forced to repress those feelings of disrespect, humiliation, and injustice, which eventually causes those feelings to fester into frustration, anger, resentment, and bitterness—far more powerful emotions than they were originally faced with. Eventually those powerful repressed emotions spill over and explode into greater levels of violence evidenced by the shootings and stabbings we see by young men across the country.

A big mistake that our culture currently makes with boys is that we unconsciously combine aggression and violence into one behavior. From a male's perspective the two are not the same. Boys and men see aggression as useful—it is *constructive* of the self. Violence is just the opposite—it is *destructive*.[3] So when our schools, courts, and social service workers confuse the two it does a disservice to boys who actually *need* aggression in many areas of their life. Our culture just generally assumes now that the more feminized traits like being quiet, sitting down, being contemplative, and nurturing are the right way to act, and the more masculine traits like anger, aggression, confrontation, and one-upmanship are wrong—in every circumstance! That's not true and does a great disservice to our boys. There *are* times when it is appropriate to be angry and confrontational instead of passive or gentle.

Our schools' and culture's knee-jerk response to male violence (or even just natural aggression) of establishing a "no tolerance" policy has probably been more detrimental than helpful to young males. (If there is any question that our public educational system has been "feminized" we need look no further than this policy.) One reason is because it's actually less frightening for a male to "act out" (physically fight) when he feels threatened than it is to have the self-control to face the issue head on. So for instance when a boy gets made fun of on the playground, his sense of honor requires him to respond. But perhaps because he does not have the maturity or coping skills to understand that the more "manly" thing to do would be to confront his attackers in a nonviolent way, he responds emotionally and strikes back. When we condemn his action or response as being "bad" we send the message that his honor is not worth fighting for. And yet he has an innate ego response mechanism that causes him to seek justice when he is disrespected. To not allow him to respond or to require he get someone else (like an adult female) to advocate for him tells him he is powerless, disrespected, and dishonorable. Respect is a key attribute of the core of a male's psyche. When he does not feel respected or is allowed to be disrespected without recourse, it rots his pride and weakens his level of self-respect.

I'm not promoting that we should teach young males that violence is the way to solve problems. But the myth that "violence never solved anything" is just that, a myth. Violence solves lots of problems—especially violent problems. If someone is trying to murder your wife and children, appealing to their sense of compassion is probably not a good strategy to stop them.

Back in the "old days" when a gym teacher had two boys who had problems with each other (which is inevitable) he put boxing gloves on them both and told them to settle their differences in a supervised environment. Afterward, they were made to shake hands and forget about it. Even in the most adversarial unsupervised playground scuffle seldom was anyone injured beyond a bloody nose. Males always respect their opponent after doing battle with one another and frequently become good friends because of the respect they earn for one another. We did not see the problems then that we face today with high levels of violence and the killing of our young men.

However, our more feminized world of total tolerance does not allow a young man to seek justice, which causes him to be resentful and angry. Males are taught it is bad to fight or even be aggressive over any insult no matter how egregious the offense. This frustrates their sense of justice.

Again, I'm not promoting violence, bullying, or unchecked aggression, but this kind of "feminization" of young males not only results in a more intensified level of aggression, but also produces passive men who often internalize this anger and frustration, which then manifests itself in passive-aggressive behavior, which can be just as destructive.

I watched this play out with a group of young males at the local high school the other day. Their horseplaying was becoming somewhat aggressive as young men are wont to do. Several teachers observed this and sounded the alarm that a "fight" was about to happen. This, of course, got all the adults in a dither, running around the building, sounding the alarm. It was obvious from the boys' reaction to this that they enjoyed the control they gained over the adults who were responding to their "gang fight." You could virtually see the gears turning in their heads as they somewhat tongue-in-cheek continued the escapades until the teachers and administration had worked themselves into a near panic, at which point the boys quietly disappeared into the sunset with smirks on their faces.

We do our boys a disservice when we do not allow them a certain amount of aggression and autonomy in solving their own social problems. Males are physical beings—they solve problems through action, not by talking about their feelings. (Frankly, to talk about your feelings after having had your honor disparaged does not seem like adequate recompense.) Males often bond with one another through aggression. This means males are biologically wired to be more physically active, more aggressive, and more likely to need physical activity to blow off emotional stress. If we want to eliminate physical aggression and fights with young males, we must find physical competitions or other direct challenges for them to engage in when they have issues with each other. This teaches them to be true warriors who use their power to lift up others, rather than becoming bullies who abuse those weaker than they are.

How to Teach Your Son to Be a Warrior-Poet

No man ever understands quite his own artful dodges to escape from the grim shadow of self-knowledge.

—Joseph Conrad, *Lord Jim*

In order to teach our sons to be warriors-poets, we must teach them two separate aspects of their character—physical and artistic. What does a warrior-poet look like? In the movie *Braveheart*, William Wallace, played by Mel Gibson, was a warrior-poet. He was adopted by his uncle after the death of his father. His uncle not only gave him a classic education but taught him warrior skills as well. He went on to lead a nation toward its freedom.

A warrior-poet is similar to a Renaissance man—he has expertise in many areas of life. Even an artisan—which you would consider to be an intellectual pursuit—such as Michelangelo showed incredible physical stamina when painting the Sistine Chapel. He would not have been able to create something so beautiful and awe-inspiring had he not had the physical capacity to do so. In fact, nearly all of the great men highlighted throughout this book had developed themselves physically as well as mentally. Perhaps it takes both aspects of a man's being in order to pull himself out of the mediocrity that most men suffer.

Let's look at a male's creative side first. I think all men have a desire in their hearts to *create* something. We have a need or craving to create something that will outlast our presence on earth—that will tell future generations, "I was here!" We even see this propensity in boys who busy themselves creating sand castles on the beach, building tree houses in the backyard, and building snowmen and forts in the winter. Some men find relief for this craving through designing and building things, some by building business empires, others by fixing things that are broken, others through creating something from nothing (even as simple as creating a fine lawn where once there was just dirt), and still others from participating in the finer arts such as acting, singing, and painting. All of these things are, to one degree or another, a form of creativity. Some activities, like sculpting, may seem more creative than say, fixing a big-block V-8 engine. But to a man who loves cars, nothing speaks to his soul more than the rumble of a finely tuned motor as it sits idling like a sleeping big cat.

Art gives us life. If you have ever had the chance to listen to a professional orchestra or a night of chamber music you know the depth of peace and joy music can give to your soul. English dramatist William Congreve even said, "Music has charms to soothe a savage beast."[4] Actually he didn't say that, it's often misquoted. What he actually said was, ". . . to soothe a savage *breast*," but you get the point. In fact, it may be even more relevant in that he means it soothes a wounded human soul or tortured heart.

There is a video from YouTube making the rounds that shows an elderly man in a nursing home, apparently living out the end of his life. He is incoherent, unresponsive, downcast, possibly exhibiting dementia. Some scientists and social workers place headphones on him and begin to play music he listened to as a younger man. The transformation is almost instantaneous. His eyes light up, he becomes engaged in the music, and he begins singing along and moving to the beat. He appears happy and vibrant. Even after removing the headphones he is able to cognitively answer questions and engage in animated conversation. His response is nearly miraculous as he transforms before your eyes from having a "tortured breast" to a soothed heart just from the nourishing music to his soul. He is alive again![5]

If we look at artistic creativity from a broader perspective than just the fine arts, it might make it easier to help our boys become more creative. The challenge when we look at artistic creativity is that not all of us are born with classic artistic skills or gifts. But interestingly, many of us are born with varying degrees of creative ability. For instance, when it comes to people or still life, I cannot draw or paint my way out of a paper bag, but my son is always asking me to draw cartoons. I seem to have a knack for drawing comics. Other men are gifted when doodling around with metal, or working with wood, or designing buildings. I have one friend who creates custom metal works. He is definitely an artist with an arc welder. Another friend is gifted when it comes to mixing music tapes. Still another makes these incredible sand sculptures at the beach during annual competitions. You wouldn't think he has a creative bone in his body to talk to him, but he can mix sand and water to make marvelous shapes. A guy in my neighborhood (whom I've been hoping to meet someday) customizes cars and trucks out of his garage. Some pretty cool designs and creations of artisan quality come rolling out of that shop.

But as Matisse said, "Creativity takes courage." Especially for boys, to expose our creative self is frightening enough, but to open ourselves up to criticism is also a bit intimidating. Even after years as a writer, I still cringe when I send manuscripts to my editor—especially the areas where I have really opened up and poured my soul onto paper. (And I trust her—we've worked together for years. Imagine how challenging it is to open ourselves up to the anonymous public.) And yet to truly satisfy our need to be creative, that is what we must do. To create something and never share it with the world is to hide our efforts under a blanket. The man (or boy) who paints a picture, or plays an instrument, or sculpts a wood carving, or builds a cedar chest and then lacks the courage to expose it to the world suffers because of it. He never gets the immense satisfaction of someone being drawn into what he creates and connecting with it on a deep "soul" level. The process of creating something and opening the opportunity for praise or criticism is empowering and part of the creative process—I think.

Budget cuts in schools are eliminating art programs for many districts across the country. This is devastating in many ways (and trust me, I'm not a huge supporter of the current state of public education). For many young people this was the only hands-on exposure to drawing, sculpting, painting, or pottery they would ever get in life. Kids from lower socio-economic backgrounds seldom get exposed to art beyond what they see on television. For boys, being forced to participate in these programs can open a new and wonderful world for them that they may not have had the courage to explore before or in any other way.

I sometimes feel sorry for art teachers. They are so passionate about their craft and yet they have to put up with so many unruly and rough young men like me and my friends. We were unknowingly afraid or intimidated by the risk of showing our vulnerability through our artistic soul (and the potential criticism that accompanied it), and so we fooled around and made fun of the process. We probably made the art teacher's life miserable. She always seemed like she was on the verge of a nervous breakdown. I'm sure in her poetic soul she could not understand why none of us were captured by the magnificence of the arts. And yet this exposure came to fruition years later and has been a blessing to my life. I became a writer, and one of the guys I used to draw cartoons with has become a world-famous artist. Without that early and ongoing exposure to art, perhaps many young men are never able to access the "velvet" part of their identity that Andelin talks about.

I would encourage you to take your son to plays, art exhibits, museums, and other culturally enriching events. Enter him in summertime painting or sculpting classes. Have him take music lessons and learn to play an instrument or take singing lessons. Or have him be part of the cast in a play one year. Exposing him to a wide variety of creative and artist activities not only enriches him personally but also exposes areas that he may develop a passion for later in life. I have several friends whose parents literally forced them to take music lessons as a boy and who now derive great joy from being able to sit down and express their mood and feelings through a musical instrument—I am so envious of them. Life's not all about football, cars, and girls. It's also not just about video games and pizza. I'm not sure how many frustrated actors or musicians there are out there making a living as CPAs or insurance salesmen, but I imagine there are more than a few.

Many boys think the arts are for "sissies." Teach your son that there is nothing feminine or unmanly about the creative process—especially if it helps bring joy to other people. Help your son become well rounded as a person by exploring his creative side—even if he doesn't want to. We need artists and poets as much as we need engineers and scientists.

On the other hand, regardless of their bent or personality, all boys should learn how to defend themselves physically—whether that involves lessons in boxing, wrestling, martial arts, or some combination of all. That's probably an unpopular notion today, but a boy who can physically defend himself walks with greater confidence. Even (or maybe especially) young males who are sensitive or somewhat uncoordinated benefit greatly from learning to be competent in self-defense. And even highly intellectual males benefit from developing their bodies as well as their minds. Teddy Roosevelt learned early in life that he needed to develop his physique as well as his brain. David was able to protect himself and those under his responsibility because he developed his physical attributes. Abe Lincoln strengthened both his mind and his body.

A warrior is required to at least be prepared to give the biggest sacrifice of all—his life for others. It's a lesson that parents and spouses need to emulate. Warriors are also familiar with and trained in most, if not all, of the traits discussed in this book: duty, courage, honor, loyalty, self-discipline, and hardihood.

As political correctness has run roughshod over our culture, we have taken away virtually anything that might inspire a boy to desire to be a warrior. Aggressiveness is discouraged if not banned. We medicate boys who show too much passion or physical rambunctiousness.

The war on masculinity has devastated boys. A man or boy learns early that to speak his mind too boldly or try to lead too passionately is to invite criticism from a variety of sources. We somehow have accepted the notion that in order to lift up girls, we've had to tear down boys. But this is not a "one or the other" proposition. We can empower both females and males to be more successful in life without its being at the expense of the other gender. This mentality has harmed both males and females.

Author and pastor Erwin McManus pointedly stated it this way: "Now, women have really fought for their equality, for their voice, for their strength, for their power, and part of that has been to make sure that men were not in the way. A part of that fight has been the diminishing of male strength and the masculine ego. But now those women need men who are as strong as they are, and I hear this question all the time from women: 'Where are the men?' And I tell them, 'Well, look under your shoe.'"[6]

I believe it is important to give boys a well-rounded education. So for every physical activity he participates in, it is important that your son develop his mental acumen as well (and vice versa). For example, if he plays a sport, make sure he learns to also play an instrument. If he is in Boy Scouts, make sure he is also learning to speak a foreign language. If he is a computer geek, make sure he also develops his body through a martial arts program. If he likes to work on cars, make sure he learns to read.

His natural inclination will be to resist whatever he is uncomfortable doing. It is important that you require him to develop both his mind and his body. If he is too heavy on one side or the other he will not be in balance and his life and the lives of those around him will suffer because of it.

But perhaps the most important gift you can give your son to help him in life is to ensure that he learns how to read and then be forced (at least encouraged) to do so consistently. So many men and boys claim to not like to read. But I think it is more an issue of never really having learned *how* to read, and so they feel like a failure and avoid it. At least I've never met a man who knew how to read who didn't like it. And the majority of men I've met who didn't like to read were not very good at it. Reading opens up whole new worlds for males and it creates men who continue to learn their entire lives. It allows them the opportunity to become warrior-poets, even if in their own minds.

Last, a warrior-poet has a highly developed faith. Faith is belief not based on proof. It is confidence in something you cannot see, hear, or smell. It is intangible, not subject to material evidence. It is loyalty, fidelity, and trust in God and his teachings. For example, I believe that there is an omnipotent God who created the universe and everything in it even though I cannot prove his existence by any scientific manner. Besides, whatever you believe, the benefits of meditation, prayer, and having a faith belief are documented and well proven.

So how do we transfer our faith to our children? We are losing our young people (especially our young men) in droves from the church. Parents spend huge amounts of time taking their children to church as they are growing up, only to find them uninterested once they get to high school or go away to college. The church invests large amounts of resources in youth ministry programs only to see the results dwindle as kids get older. Many churches do not even have a college age group program, as no young people that age go to their church.

If we are to raise "exceptional" human beings, then we have to expect greater challenges. Anything worth doing in life is difficult. In addition, if a person's destiny is such that he will make a positive impact on the world, the Evil One will not be likely to sit by and be content to allow that to happen.

As my wife and I mentor and do premarital counseling with young couples, we occasionally come across some that are exceptional. Both individuals have lived a worthy life and have prepared themselves to live what I would consider a superior life—one that uses its power and gifts to lift up the lives of others. Truly I can see God's hand upon these young men and women and can envision what God is going to accomplish through their union. These

How to Inspire Boys to Stay in Church

Church can be boring for boys—especially churches focused toward a feminine perspective of worship. In order to keep boys interested we need to attract men (and manly men). Fortunately, the same things that attract boys keep the interest of men as well. Here are some ideas and questions to ask yourself:

1. Are the foyer and sanctuary masculine-friendly, or do they look like the inside of a day spa?
2. Does your church have *healthy* masculine leadership? If men are gladly coming it probably does—if not it probably doesn't. Does the church have an active, vibrant men's group that does outdoor activities with boys?
3. Is the worship service exciting? Many males prefer older hymns that have strong words of faith and bold action. Some newer worship songs that drone on and on about Jesus being the "lover of my soul" make males uncomfortable.
4. Do the church leaders encourage passionate (i.e., mistake-making) male leaders or only timid, passive, "nice" men who act perfect?
5. Does the youth group study the great heroic stories of the Bible (David and Goliath, Samson, Daniel, Joshua and Caleb, or the fiery furnace boys—Shadrach, Meshach, and Abednego) or do they focus on only a meek and mild, turn-the-other-cheek Jesus?
6. Is your church men's ministry *doing* things (helping single moms with fix-it projects, feeding the homeless, working on cars for elderly people, establishing fatherless boy programs, etc.)? Also, does the men's group take boys through discipleship programs such as Men's Fraternity, Wild at Heart, or Better Dads Stronger Sons? Young males thrive under mentoring from older males.
7. Does your church take risks, or is it "safe"?

young couples are always shocked and stunned by the level of difficulties they encounter on the way to the altar. I have to explain to them that they are not "average," so why should they expect "average" problems?

In all likelihood, the fact that they experience unique problems *is normal* for them. They should anticipate a greater degree of spiritual hostility directed toward them. The fact that they face these degrees of problems may even be an indicator of their exceptionalism and the plan God has for their life. The ability to overcome these challenges hones and polishes their gifts and the strength of their relationship to prepare them for the future great deeds that God has planned for their lives. When we do exceptional things in life, we must expect a greater level of spiritual warfare. Sometimes it's hard to remember this in the heat of battle. By looking at the bigger picture it helps us to not get bogged down by the ferocity of these attacks. Life is plenty difficult anyway. But perhaps if we are raising exceptional children whom God intends to use, we should expect the spiritual attacks to be fiercer and more difficult to overcome. Why is it we see so many pastors' children rebel and turn away from the church? Is it because the parents are bad parents? Maybe it is in some cases. But I suspect it has more to do with evil influences, rebellious spirits, and spiritual warfare than with bad parenting.

Many, many boys and young men today are falling away from the church. Some statistics say that about 70 percent of young men stop attending church after high school. Understandably, parents who have dedicated their lives to the admonition of Proverbs 22:6 (NIV 1984)—"Train a child in the way he should go, and when he is old he will not turn from it"—are heartbroken when that happens. As Christians, we are often tempted to judge the parents of prodigal sons and daughters. We somehow think that the path the child chooses to walk is strictly determined by the type of parenting they were subject to. But if our children do not stray we should more likely be of the attitude, "But for the grace of God, there goes my child." As parents we have a tendency to assume guilt far too easily for the way our children turn out in life. But I've seen too many children I know who were parented well make bad life choices, and I've seen even more who were badly abused and yet turned out to be wonderful, productive people.

Much like God has given each parent free will, he has also given our children free will. That free will involves not only whether or not they accept Christ into their hearts, but also the type of walk they choose for their lives. Another aspect to that proverb—one that we do not consider very often—is that no time limit is imposed upon it. I've seen many young people walk away from the church and their faith only to come back to them later in life. Billy Graham, perhaps the greatest Christian of the twentieth century, had a child who strayed. Franklin Graham was an admitted rebellious carouser before returning to his faith and dedicating his life to serving God. I suppose Billy Graham thanks God he was alive to see the return of his prodigal son.

So no matter how difficult it may seem, I want to encourage you to stay the course. Continue to live your life with the values you think are important. Continue to force your son, if he is living under your roof, to live by the standards and boundaries that mirror your faith. Continue to love the sinner and hate the sin. Continue to lead by example. Continue to pray for your children.

Some Final Thoughts

Small boys become big men through the influence of
big men who care about small boys.

—UNKNOWN

THROUGHOUT THIS BOOK I USED MEN OF HISTORY TO
define certain character traits that I believe to be important
in developing healthy male leadership. These are not the
only traits that we should teach our sons, but they're an excellent
place to begin. I used men as examples and not women because
this book is written to try to develop our *sons* to become leaders of their families and their communities. Masculinity bestows
masculinity. Boys learn best under the tutelage and modeling of
men, so it seemed *apropos* to use male role models. I gave a brief
biography of each man I used. I intentionally focused on the positive contributions they made to society and less on their foibles.
No human male is perfect, and neither were any of these men.

That said, as parents you have the greatest influence on your
children of anybody on the planet. So many parents are concerned
about outside influences, but study after study shows that the people

with the most influence in a child's life (even teenagers) are their parents.

It's a stereotype that teenagers do not want to spend time with their parents. Studies show that kids who spend time with their fathers have better self-esteem and better interpersonal communication skills.[1]

But that means that we have to be willing to and courageous enough to actually use that influence. If we are absent too often or are afraid to exert our values and ideals onto our children, we lose that influence and waste the opportunity to teach them valuable life lessons.

And lest we forget, a mother and father working together are more powerful than any individual parent. When a man and a woman use each others' strengths to compensate for each partner's weaknesses, then they become much more powerful as a team than they are as individuals. I encourage you as a team to develop a plan to intentionally teach your values to your children. Oftentimes when we react (instead of being proactive) to life, we miss or mishandle teaching moments. Your sons (and daughters) need all your help and experiences in order to successfully become the men (and women) that God created them to be.

Bonne chance et allez avec Dieu.

Acknowledgments

I'D LIKE TO ACKNOWLEDGE AND THANK THE MANY MEN throughout the country who are selflessly working to mentor boys. These men seldom get credit for their efforts. They are heroes but never make the headlines. They sacrifice their time, energy, and knowledge, while seldom seeing their efforts come to fruition. I shudder to think what would become of many of these boys without these men and their valiant efforts. These men are too many to mention, and I apologize in advance for those of you who I left out, but to name just a few of you . . .

Tony Rorie of Men of Honor, John Smithbaker of Fathers in the Field, Sam Mehaffie of Saving Our Boys, Kenneth Braswell of Fathers, Inc., Jeff Purkiss of Squires2Knights Ministries, Gary Randle and Noble Crawford of H.O.P.E. Farm, John Sowers of The Mentoring Project, all of the leaders in programs such as the Boy Scouts of America, and all the men who are now and have been involved in the past with our Better Dads Standing Tall mentoring programs.

Please know that all of the mothers of those boys (and perhaps even the boys themselves) have been praying to God for his help.

God chose you men as answers to people's prayers. Your work is eternal. You may not see the rewards of your gallant behavior while on earth, but someday in heaven you will be eternally blessed to meet all the people in whose lives you have made a difference. May God bless you and protect you.

Notes

Boys to Men

1. C. S. Lewis, *The Abolition of Man* (New York: Macmillan, 1947), 78.
2. "Great Man Theory," *Wikipedia*, http://en.wikipedia.org/wiki/Great_Man_theory, accessed 8/14/2011.

Chapter 1 Courage

1. Brett and Kate McKay, *The Art of Manliness Manvotionals: Timeless Wisdom and Advice on Living the 7 Manly Virtues* (Cincinnati, OH: How Books, 2011), 39.
2. Stephen B. Oates, *Let the Trumpet Sound: A Life of Martin Luther King, Jr.* (New York: HarperPerennial, 1994), 159.
3. Portions of the biographies in this book have been drawn from sources in *Wikipedia*.
4. Henry Van Dyke, *Manhood, Faith, and Courage* (1906), as quoted in McKay, *Art of Manliness Manvotionals*, 42–43.
5. "Billy Graham Quotes," Thinkexist.com, http://thinkexist.com/quotation/courage_is_contagious-when_a_brave_man_takes_a/200524.html, accessed 8/9/12.
6. Michael Gurian, *How Do I Help Him? A Practitioner's Guide to Working with Boys and Men in Therapeutic Settings* (Spokane, WA: Gurian Institute Press, 2011), 100.
7. "sheeple," *Wikipedia*, http://en.wikipedia.org/wiki/Sheeple, accessed 3/4/12.

Chapter 2 Honor and Nobility

1. McKay, *The Art of Manliness Manvotionals,* 2.
2. Ibid., 2.
3. Gleaned from Roy Blount Jr., *Robert E. Lee* (New York: Penguin Putnam, 2003).

4. H. W. Crocker III, *Robert E. Lee on Leadership: Executive Lessons in Character, Courage, and Vision* (Roseville, CA: Prima Publishing, 1999) 35, 52.

5. Ibid., 32.

6. Professor Edward S. Joynes, chair of Modern Languages at Washington College under Lee, originally published in *Richmond Dispatch*, January 27, 1901.

7. Clint Johnson, *The Politically Incorrect Guide to the South (and Why It Will Rise Again)* (Washington, DC: Regnery Publishing, 2006), 165.

8. Orison Swett Marden, *Success* (magazine), originally founded in 1897, quoted in http://artofmanliness.com/2010/11/13/manvotional-robert-e-lees-chivalry/.

9. "Robert E. Lee Biography," SonoftheSouth.net, http://www.sonofthesouth.net/leefoundation/About%20the%20General.htm.

10. Lewis, *Abolition of Man*, 35.

11. Google Books, *The Abolition of Man* review, http://books.google.com/books/about/The_Abolition_of_Man_Or_Reflections_on_E.html?id=ST87o-KSzp0c, accessed 3/9/12.

Chapter 3 Duty

1. Laurie Calkhoven, *George Washington: An American Life* (New York: Sterling Publishing Co., 2006), chaps. 1–2.

2. Ibid., 24–25.

3. George Washington bio, http://sc94.ameslab.gov/tour/gwash.html.

4. Ibid., 45–46.

5. Calkhoven, *George Washington*, 58.

6. Aubrey Andelin, *Man of Steel and Velvet* (Pierce City, MO: Pacific Press Santa Barbara ed., 1972), 38–39.

7. Previous five paragraphs gleaned from conversations with David McLaughlin, creator of Role of a Man seminars.

Chapter 4 Integrity and Loyalty

1. The Official Site of Coach John Wooden, http://www.coachwooden.com/.

2. Pat Williams with Jim Denney, *Coach Wooden: The Seven Principles That Shaped His Life and Will Change Yours* (Grand Rapids: Revell, 2011), 167.

3. "John Wooden Obituary," Legacy.com, http://www.legacy.com/NS/Obituary.aspx?pid=143327829, accessed 3/20/12.

4. Williams with Denney, *Coach Wooden*, 26.

5. Ibid., 55.

6. John Wooden with Steve Jamison, *Wooden: A Lifetime of Observations and Reflections On and Off the Court* (Chicago: Contemporary Books, 1997), 18.

7. John Wooden, *They Call Me Coach* (New York: McGraw-Hill, 2003), 95.

Chapter 5 Self-Discipline

1. "Discipline," *Wikipedia*, http://en.wikipedia.org/wiki/Discipline, accessed 5/8/12.

2. Edmund Morris, *The Rise of Theodore Roosevelt* (New York: The Modern Library, 1979), 11–12.

3. Ibid., 32.
4. McKay, *Art of Manliness Manvotionals*, 187.
5. "Research," *Prison Studies Project*, http://prisonstudiesproject.org/research/, accessed 5/21/12.
6. Gurian, *How Do I Help Him?*, 73.
7. Ibid., 85–87.
8. Morris, *Rise of Theodore Roosevelt*, 13.
9. Williams with Denney, *Coach Wooden*, 140.
10. Andelin, *Man of Steel and Velvet*, 99.
11. Ibid., 85–102.

Chapter 6 Perseverance

1. Steven Otfinoski, *Abraham Lincoln* (New York: Children's Press, 2004), 8–12.
2. Williams with Denney, *Coach Wooden*, 79.
3. Edwin Louis Cole, *Never Quit* (Southlake, TX: Watercolor Books, 1993), 44.
4. Williams with Denney, *Coach Wooden*, 132.
5. Randy Alcorn, *90 Days of God's Goodness* (Colorado Springs: Multnomah, 2011), 198.
6. Ralph Waldo Emerson, "Heroism." *Essays, First Series*, 1841, quoted in McKay, *Art of Manliness Manvotionals*, 60.
7. Cole, *Never Quit*, 37.
8. ABC News, "Persistence Is Learned from Fathers, Says Study," June 15, 2012, http://abcnews.go.com/Health/persistence-learned-fathers-study/story?id=16571927#.T99LTI7lPZF.

Chapter 7 Hardihood and Resiliency

1. Brett and Kate McKay, "Manvotional: Do You Have Hardihood?" *Art of Manliness* website, January 17, 2010, http://artofmanliness.com/2010/01/17/manvotional-do-you-have-hardihood/.
2. "Jedediah Smith," *Wikipedia*, http://en.wikipedia.org/wiki/Jedediah_Smith, accessed 3/2/12.
3. Ibid.
4. Andelin, *Man of Steel and Velvet*, 3.
5. Ibid., 15.
6. Conn Iggulden and Hal Iggulden, *The Dangerous Book for Boys* (New York: HarperCollins, 2007), 75–78.
7. Gurian, *How Do I Help Him?*, 67.
8. Ibid., 90.
9. William A. Alcott, *The Young Man's Guide* (Boston, MA: Perkins and Marvin, 1836), 2–3.

Chapter 8 Common Sense and Wisdom

1. "Wisdom," *Wikipedia*, http://en.wikipedia.org/wiki/Wisdom, accessed 2/23/12.
2. Ryan J. Ferrier, "4 Ways to Pour Yourself into Your Pursuits," Michael Hyatt Blog, http://michaelhyatt.com/, accessed 6/22/12.

3. "Inventor," *The Franklin Institute*, http://fi.edu/franklin/inventor/inventor.html.
4. Ibid.
5. Edwin Louis Cole, *Real Man* (Southlake, TX: Watercolor Books, 1992), 19.
6. Eric Reed, "The Demise of Guys? Boys' Brains Are Being Rewired by Video Games and Online Porn," *Leadership Journal*, Nov. 10, 2011, http://www.outofur.com/archives/2011/11/the_demise_of_g.html.
7. Michael Gurian with Terry Trueman, *What Stories Does My Son Need?* (New York: Jeremy P. Tarcher/Putnam, 2000), 5, 7.
8. Gurian, *How Do I Help Him?*, 44–45.
9. Ibid., 34–39.
10. Ibid.
11. Ibid.
12. Ibid., 34–54.
13. Ibid., 54–59.

Chapter 9 Vision

1. Rita Thievon Mullin, *Thomas Jefferson: Architect of Freedom* (New York: Sterling Publishing Co., 2007), 6.
2. Jacqueline Ching, *Thomas Jefferson: A Photographic Story of a Life* (New York: DK Publishing, 2009), 24.

Chapter 10 Intellect

1. Henry Morris, *Men of Science Men of God* (Green Forest, AZ: Master Books, 1988), http://www.answersingenesis.org/articles/1998/03/02/leonardo-da-vinci.
2. Mario Lucertini, Ana Millán Gasca, and F. Nicolò, eds., *Technological Concepts and Mathematical Models in the Evolution of Modern Engineering* (Berlin, Germany: Birkhäuser, 2004), 13.
3. Mark Sherman, "We Owe to Our Sons What We've Given to Our Daughters," Real Men Don't Write Blogs, *Psychology Today*, February 13, 2013, http://www.psychologytoday.com/em/118117.
4. Gurian, *How Do I Help Him?*, 15.
5. Nick Szymanis, "Boys at School: Is It the Teaching or the Tests?" *Globe and Mail*, Dec. 12, 2011, http://www.theglobeandmail.com/news/opinions/opinion/boys-at-school-is-it-the-teaching-or-the-tests/article2266450/.
6. C. S. Lewis, *The Abolition of Man*, 32–33.
7. Peter Marshall and David Manuel, *The Light and the Glory* (Grand Rapids: Revell, 1977), 435.
8. Seth Godin, *Stop Stealing Dreams*, Ebook, 2012, 14, http://www.sethgodin.com/sg/docs/StopStealingDreamsSCREEN.pdf.
9. Gurian, *How Do I Help Him?*, 121.
10. Ibid., 122.
11. Alan Fram, "One in Four Read No Books Last Year," *Washington Post*, August 21, 2007, http://www.washingtonpost.com/wp-dyn/content/article/2007/08/21/AR2007082101045.html.

12. For a more complete study on this, see Michael Gurian, *Boys and Girls Learn Differently!* (San Francisco: Jossey-Bass, 2001).

Chapter 11 Compassion and Empathy

1. C. S. Lewis, *The Abolition of Man*, 34.
2. "Respect and Responsibility: The Truth About Kids Who Hunt," produced by Randall Eaton, PhD, DVD recording, 1997.
3. Randall Eaton, *From Boys to Men of Heart: Hunting as a Rite of Passage* (Shelton, WA: OWLink Media, 2009), xlix.
4. Ibid.

Chapter 12 Warrior-Poet

1. Online Metals Weight Calculator, OnlineMetals.com, http://www.onlinemetals .com/calculator.cfm, accessed 3/7/12.
2. Heather Turgeon, "Low Sperm Count: Why Male Fertility is Falling," *The Daily Beast*, Jan. 4, 2011, http://www.thedailybeast.com/articles/2011/01/04/low-sperm-count-why-male-fertility-is-falling.html, accessed 1/4/2011.
3. Gurian, *How Do I Help Him?*, 108.
4. William Congreve, *The Mourning Bride*, 1697, quoted in "Music Has Charms to Soothe the Savage Beast," *The Phrase Finder*, http://www.phrases.org.uk/meanings /252000.html.
5. "Old Man in Nursing Home Reacts to Hearing Music from His Era," http:// www.youtube.com/watch?v=NKDXuCE7LeQ.
6. Interview with Erwin McManus, by Carter Phipps, "Awaken the Poet Warrior," *EnlightenNext Magazine*, Aug.–Oct. 2008, http://www.enlightennext.org/ magazine/j41/mcmanus.asp?page=2.

Some Final Thoughts

1. "Why Teens Should Spend Time with Dads," CNN.com, http://www.cnn. com/video/?/video/bestoftv/2012/08/26/levs-teen-stereotypes.cnn#/video/bestoftv /2012/08/26/levs-teen-stereotypes.cnn.

Rick Johnson is a bestselling author of *That's My Son*; *That's My Teenage Son*; *That's My Girl*; *Better Dads, Stronger Sons*; and *Becoming Your Spouse's Better Half*. He is the founder of Better Dads and is a sought-after speaker at many large parenting and marriage conferences across the United States and Canada. Rick, his wife, Suzanne, and their grown children live in Oregon. To find out more about Rick Johnson, visit www.betterdads.net.

Meet

RICK JOHNSON

at www.BetterDads.net

Connect with Rick on Facebook

 *Rick Johnson*

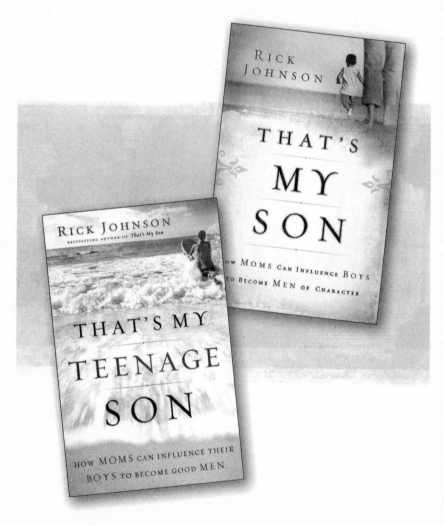

ENCOURAGEMENT FOR FATHERS IN THEIR MOST IMPORTANT ROLE

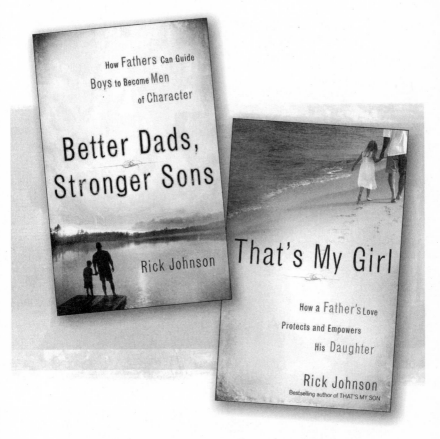

Parenting expert Rick Johnson's plainspoken common sense, humor, and advice will give you the confidence and the encouragement you need to take up the active, positive role that can change your child's life—starting now.

YOUR RECIPE FOR MARITAL SUCCESS

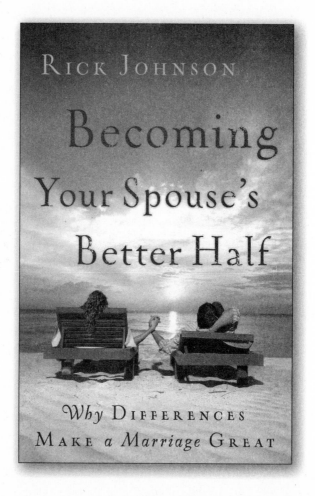

Learn how to use your differences to add spice and passion to your marriage.